CAMBRIDGE
UNIVERSITY PRESS

CAMBRIDGE ENGLISH
Language Assessment
Part of the University of Cambridge

Cambridge English

OFFICIAL

CAMBRIDGE PREPARATION MATERIAL

IELTS 11
ACADEMIC

WITH ANSWERS

AUTHENTIC EXAMINATION PAPERS

Cambridge University Press
www.cambridge.org/elt

Cambridge English Language Assessment
www.cambridgeenglish.org

Information on this title: www.cambridge.org/9781316503850

© Cambridge University Press and UCLES 2016

First published 2016

Printed in China by CNPIEC Beijing Congreat Printing Co., Ltd.

A catalogue record for this publication is available from the British Library
ISBN 978-1-316-61230-9 General Training Student's Book with answers with Audio China reprint edition
ISBN 978-1-316-50397-3 General Training Student's Book with answers with Audio
ISBN 978-1-316-50388-1 General Training Student's Book with answer
ISBN 978-1-316-61225-5 Academic Student's Book with answers with Audio for New Oriental School China reprint edition
ISBN 978-1-316-61223-1 Academic Student's Book with answers with Audio China reprint edition
ISBN 978-1-316-50385-0 Academic Student's Book with answers
ISBN 978-1-316-50396-6 Academic Student's Book with answers with Audio
ISBN 978-1-316-50392-8 Audio CDs (2)

Contents

Introduction

The International English Language Testing System (IELTS) is widely recognised as a reliable means of assessing the language ability of candidates who need to study or work where English is the language of communication. These Practice Tests are designed to give future IELTS candidates an idea of whether their English is at the required level.

IELTS is owned by three partners, Cambridge English Language Assessment, part of the University of Cambridge, the British Council and IDP Education Pty Limited (through its subsidiary company, IELTS Australia Pty Limited). Further information on IELTS can be found on the IELTS website www.ielts.org.

WHAT IS THE TEST FORMAT?

IELTS consists of four components. All candidates take the same Listening and Speaking tests. There is a choice of Reading and Writing tests according to whether a candidate is taking the Academic or General Training module.

Academic	General Training
For candidates wishing to study at undergraduate or postgraduate levels, and for those seeking professional registration.	For candidates wishing to migrate to an English-speaking country (Australia, Canada, New Zealand, UK), and for those wishing to train or study at below degree level.

The test components are taken in the following order:

Listening		
4 sections, 40 items approximately 30 minutes		
Academic Reading 3 sections, 40 items 60 minutes	or	**General Training Reading** 3 sections, 40 items 60 minutes
Academic Writing 2 tasks 60 minutes	or	**General Training Writing** 2 tasks 60 minutes
Speaking 11 to 14 minutes		
Total Test Time 2 hours 44 minutes		

ACADEMIC TEST FORMAT

Listening

This test consists of four sections, each with ten questions. The first two sections are concerned with social needs. The first section is a conversation between two speakers and the second section is a monologue. The final two sections are concerned with situations related to educational or training contexts. The third section is a conversation between up to four people and the fourth section is a monologue.

A variety of question types is used, including: multiple choice, matching, plan/map/diagram labelling, form completion, note completion, table completion, flow-chart completion, summary completion, sentence completion, short-answer questions.

Candidates hear the recording once only and answer the questions as they listen. Ten minutes are allowed at the end for candidates to transfer their answers to the answer sheet.

Reading

This test consists of three sections with 40 questions. There are three texts, which are taken from journals, books, magazines and newspapers. The texts are on topics of general interest. At least one text contains detailed logical argument.

A variety of question types is used, including: multiple choice, identifying information (True/False/Not Given), identifying the writer's views/claims (Yes/No/Not Given), matching information, matching headings, matching features, matching sentence endings, sentence completion, summary completion, note completion, table completion, flow-chart completion, diagram label completion, short-answer questions.

Writing

This test consists of two tasks. It is suggested that candidates spend about 20 minutes on Task 1, which requires them to write at least 150 words, and 40 minutes on Task 2, which requires them to write at least 250 words. Task 2 contributes twice as much as Task 1 to the Writing score.

Task 1 requires candidates to look at a diagram or some data (graph, table or chart) and to present the information in their own words. They are assessed on their ability to organise, present and possibly compare data, describe the stages of a process, describe an object or event, or explain how something works.

In Task 2, candidates are presented with a point of view, argument or problem. They are assessed on their ability to present a solution to the problem, present and justify an opinion, compare and contrast evidence and opinions, evaluate and challenge ideas, evidence or arguments.

Candidates are also assessed on their ability to write in an appropriate style.

More information on assessing the Writing test, including Writing Assessment Criteria (public version), is available on the IELTS website.

Speaking

This test takes between 11 and 14 minutes and is conducted by a trained examiner. There are three parts:

Part 1

The candidate and the examiner introduce themselves. Candidates then answer general questions about themselves, their home/family, their job/studies, their interests and a wide range of similar familiar topic areas. This part lasts between four and five minutes.

Part 2

The candidate is given a task card with prompts and is asked to talk on a particular topic. The candidate has one minute to prepare and they can make some notes if they wish, before speaking for between one and two minutes. The examiner then asks one or two questions on the same topic.

Part 3

The examiner and the candidate engage in a discussion of more abstract issues which are thematically linked to the topic in Part 2. The discussion lasts between four and five minutes.

The Speaking test assesses whether candidates can communicate effectively in English. The assessment takes into account Fluency and Coherence, Lexical Resource, Grammatical Range and Accuracy, and Pronunciation. More information on assessing the Speaking test, including Speaking Assessment Criteria (public version), is available on the IELTS website.

HOW IS IELTS SCORED?

IELTS results are reported on a nine-band scale. In addition to the score for overall language ability, IELTS provides a score in the form of a profile for each of the four skills (Listening, Reading, Writing and Speaking). These scores are also reported on a nine-band scale. All scores are recorded on the Test Report Form along with details of the candidate's nationality, first language and date of birth. Each Overall Band Score corresponds to a descriptive statement which gives a summary of the English language ability of a candidate classified at that level. The nine bands and their descriptive statements are as follows:

9 **Expert User** – *Has fully operational command of the language: appropriate, accurate and fluent with complete understanding.*

8 **Very Good User** – *Has fully operational command of the language with only occasional unsystematic inaccuracies and inappropriacies. Misunderstandings may occur in unfamiliar situations. Handles complex detailed argumentation well.*

7 **Good User** – *Has operational command of the language, though with occasional inaccuracies, inappropriacies and misunderstandings in some situations. Generally handles complex language well and understands detailed reasoning.*

6 **Competent User** – *Has generally effective command of the language despite some inaccuracies, inappropriacies and misunderstandings. Can use and understand fairly complex language, particularly in familiar situations.*

5 **Modest User** – *Has partial command of the language, coping with overall meaning in most situations, though is likely to make many mistakes. Should be able to handle basic communication in own field.*

4 **Limited User** – *Basic competence is limited to familiar situations. Has frequent problems in understanding and expression. Is not able to use complex language.*

3 **Extremely Limited User** – *Conveys and understands only general meaning in very familiar situations. Frequent breakdowns in communication occur.*

2 **Intermittent User** – *No real communication is possible except for the most basic information using isolated words or short formulae in familiar situations and to meet immediate needs. Has great difficulty understanding spoken and written English.*

1 **Non User** – *Essentially has no ability to use the language beyond possibly a few isolated words.*

0 **Did not attempt the test** – *No assessable information provided.*

MARKING THE PRACTICE TESTS

Listening and Reading

The Answer Keys are on pages 124–131.
Each question in the Listening and Reading tests is worth one mark.

Questions which require letter / Roman numeral answers

- For questions where the answers are letters or Roman numerals, you should write *only* the number of answers required. For example, if the answer is a single letter or numeral you should write only one answer. If you have written more letters or numerals than are required, the answer must be marked wrong.

Questions which require answers in the form of words or numbers

- Answers may be written in upper or lower case.
- Words in brackets are *optional* – they are correct, but not necessary.
- Alternative answers are separated by a slash (/).
- If you are asked to write an answer using a certain number of words and/or (a) number(s), you will be penalised if you exceed this. For example, if a question specifies an answer using NO MORE THAN THREE WORDS and the correct answer is 'black leather coat', the answer 'coat of black leather' is *incorrect*.
- In questions where you are expected to complete a gap, you should only transfer the necessary missing word(s) onto the answer sheet. For example, to complete 'in the ...', and the correct answer is 'morning', the answer 'in the morning' would be *incorrect*.
- All answers require correct spelling (including words in brackets).
- Both US and UK spelling are acceptable and are included in the Answer Key.
- All standard alternatives for numbers, dates and currencies are acceptable.
- All standard abbreviations are acceptable.
- You will find additional notes about individual answers in the Answer Key.

Writing

The sample answers are on pages 132–139. It is not possible for you to give yourself a mark for the Writing tasks. We have provided sample answers (written by candidates), showing their score and the examiner's comments. These sample answers will give you an insight into what is required for the Writing test.

HOW SHOULD YOU INTERPRET YOUR SCORES?

At the end of each Listening and Reading Answer Key you will find a chart which will help you assess whether, on the basis of your Practice Test results, you are ready to take the IELTS test.

In interpreting your score, there are a number of points you should bear in mind. Your performance in the real IELTS test will be reported in two ways: there will be a Band Score from 1 to 9 for each of the components and an Overall Band Score from 1 to 9, which is the average of your scores in the four components. However, institutions considering your application are advised to look at both the Overall Band Score and the Bands for each component in order to determine whether you have the language skills needed for a particular course of study. For example, if your course has a lot of reading and writing, but no lectures, listening skills might be less important and a score of 5 in Listening might be acceptable if the Overall Band Score was 7. However, for a course which has lots of lectures and spoken instructions, a score of 5 in Listening might be unacceptable even though the Overall Band Score was 7.

Once you have marked your tests, you should have some idea of whether your listening and reading skills are good enough for you to try the IELTS test. If you did well enough in one component, but not in others, you will have to decide for yourself whether you are ready to take the test.

The Practice Tests have been checked to ensure that they are of approximately the same level of difficulty as the real IELTS test. However, we cannot guarantee that your score in the Practice Tests will be reflected in the real IELTS test. The Practice Tests can only give you an idea of your possible future performance and it is ultimately up to you to make decisions based on your score.

Different institutions accept different IELTS scores for different types of courses. We have based our recommendations on the average scores which the majority of institutions accept. The institution to which you are applying may, of course, require a higher or lower score than most other institutions.

Further information

For more information about IELTS or any other Cambridge English Language Assessment examination, write to:

Cambridge English Language Assessment
1 Hills Road
Cambridge
CB1 2EU
United Kingdom

https://support.cambridgeenglish.org
http://www.ielts.org

Test 1

SECTION 1   Questions 1–10

Complete the notes below.

*Write **ONE WORD AND/OR A NUMBER** for each answer.*

HIRING A PUBLIC ROOM

Example

- the Main Hall – seats ....200...........

Room and cost

- the 1 .... Room – seats 100
- Cost of Main Hall for Saturday evening: **2** £ 115
  + £250 deposit (**3** .... payment is required)
- Cost includes use of tables and chairs and also **4** ....
- Additional charge for use of the kitchen: £25

Before the event

- Will need a **5** ....music........ licence
- Need to contact caretaker (Mr Evans) in advance to arrange
  6 .... entry

During the event

- The building is no smoking *rather than stage*
- The band should use the **7** .... door at the back
- Don't touch the system that controls the volume
- For microphones, contact the caretaker

10

After the event

- Need to know the 8 ~~Code~~ .... for the cleaning cupboard 不像柜
- The 9 ....~~floor~~........ must be washed and rubbish placed in black bags
- All 10 .... must be taken down
- Chairs and tables must be piled up

straightforward 简单的

he'll sort that out with you. 他会和你一起解决

entry 进入登记

detergent 清洁剂

presume 假设

SECTION 2   *Questions 11–20*

Questions 11–14

Complete the notes below.

*Write **ONE WORD** for each answer.*

Fiddy Working Heritage Farm

Advice about visiting the farm

Visitors should

- take care not to harm any **11** ....
- not touch any **12** ....
- wear **13** ....
- not bring **14** .... into the farm, with certain exceptions

Questions 15–20

Label the map below.

*Write the correct letter **A–I**, next to Questions 15–20.*

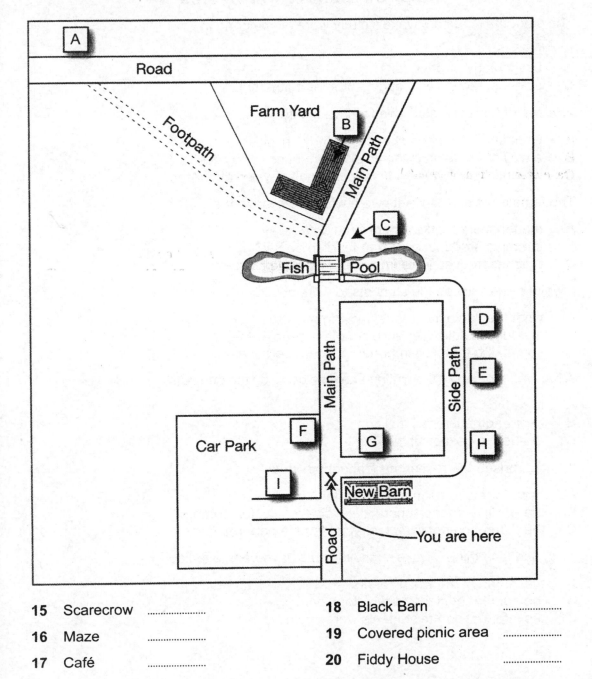

15	Scarecrow	....	**18**	Black Barn	....
16	Maze	....	**19**	Covered picnic area	....
17	Café	....	**20**	Fiddy House	....

SECTION 3   *Questions 21–30*

Choose the correct letter, **A, B** *or* **C**.

Study on Gender in Physics

21 The students in Akira Miyake's study were all majoring in

   A   physics.
   B   psychology or physics.
   C   science, technology, engineering or mathematics.

22 The aim of Miyake's study was to investigate

   A   what kind of women choose to study physics.
   B   a way of improving women's performance in physics.
   C   whether fewer women than men study physics at college.

23 The female physics students were wrong to believe that

   A   the teachers marked them in an unfair way.
   B   the male students expected them to do badly.
   C   their test results were lower than the male students'.

24 Miyake's team asked the students to write about

   A   what they enjoyed about studying physics.
   B   the successful experiences of other people.
   C   something that was important to them personally.

25 What was the aim of the writing exercise done by the subjects?

   A   to reduce stress
   B   to strengthen verbal ability
   C   to encourage logical thinking

26 What surprised the researchers about the study?

   A   how few students managed to get A grades
   B   the positive impact it had on physics results for women
   C   the difference between male and female performance

27 Greg and Lisa think Miyake's results could have been affected by

   A   the length of the writing task.
   B   the number of students who took part.
   C   the information the students were given.

28 Greg and Lisa decide that in their own project, they will compare the effects of

    A   two different writing tasks.
    B   a writing task with an oral task.
    C   two different oral tasks.

29 The main finding of Smolinsky's research was that class teamwork activities

    A   were most effective when done by all-women groups.
    B   had no effect on the performance of men or women.
    C   improved the results of men more than of women.

30 What will Lisa and Greg do next?

    A   talk to a professor
    B   observe a science class
    C   look at the science timetable

SECTION 4   *Questions 31–40*

Complete the notes below.

Write ONE WORD ONLY for each answer.

Ocean Biodiversity

Biodiversity hotspots

- areas containing many different species
- important for locating targets for **31** ....
- at first only identified on land

Boris Worm, 2005

- identified hotspots for large ocean predators, e.g. sharks
- found that ocean hotspots:
    - were not always rich in **32** ....
    - had higher temperatures at the **33** ....
    - had sufficient **34** .... in the water

Lisa Ballance, 2007

- looked for hotspots for marine **35** ....
- found these were all located where ocean currents meet

Census of Marine Life

- found new ocean species living:
    - under the **36** ....
    - near volcanoes on the ocean floor

Global Marine Species Assessment

- want to list endangered ocean species, considering:

    - population size

    - geographical distribution

    - rate of **37** ....

- Aim: to assess 20,000 species and make a distribution **38** .... for each one

Recommendations to retain ocean biodiversity

- increase the number of ocean reserves

- establish **39** .... corridors (e.g. for turtles)

- reduce fishing quotas

- catch fish only for the purpose of **40** ....

READING

READING PASSAGE 1

*You should spend about 20 minutes on **Questions 1–13**, which are based on Reading Passage 1 below.*

Crop-growing skyscrapers

By the year 2050, nearly 80% of the Earth's population will live in urban centres. Applying the most conservative estimates to current demographic trends, the human population will increase by about three billion people by then. An estimated 10^9 hectares of new land (about 20% larger than Brazil) will be needed to grow enough food to feed them, if traditional farming methods continue as they are practised today. At present, throughout the world, over 80% of the land that is suitable for raising crops is in use. Historically, some 15% of that has been laid waste by poor management practices. What can be done to ensure enough food for the world's population to live on?

The concept of indoor farming is not new, since hothouse production of tomatoes and other produce has been in vogue for some time. What is new is the urgent need to scale up this technology to accommodate another three billion people. Many believe an entirely new approach to indoor farming is required, employing cutting-edge technologies. One such proposal is for the 'Vertical Farm'. The concept is of multi-storey buildings in which food crops are grown in environmentally controlled conditions. Situated in the heart of urban centres, they would drastically reduce the amount of transportation required to bring food to consumers. Vertical farms would need to be efficient, cheap to construct and safe to operate. If successfully implemented, proponents claim, vertical farms offer the promise of urban renewal, sustainable production of a safe and varied food supply (through year-round production of all crops), and the eventual repair of ecosystems that have been sacrificed for horizontal farming.

It took humans 10,000 years to learn how to grow most of the crops we now take for granted. Along the way, we despoiled most of the land we worked, often turning verdant, natural ecozones into semi-arid deserts. Within that same time frame, we evolved into an urban species, in which 60% of the human population now lives vertically in cities. This means that, for the majority, we humans have shelter from the elements, yet we subject our food-bearing plants to the rigours of the great outdoors and can do no more than hope for a good weather year. However, more often than not now, due to a rapidly changing climate, that is not what happens. Massive floods, long droughts, hurricanes and severe monsoons take their toll each year, destroying millions of tons of valuable crops.

The supporters of vertical farming claim many potential advantages for the system. For instance, crops would be produced all year round, as they would be kept in artificially controlled, optimum growing conditions. There would be no weather-related crop failures due to droughts, floods or pests. All the food could be grown organically, eliminating the need for herbicides, pesticides and fertilisers. The system would greatly reduce the incidence of many infectious diseases that are acquired at the agricultural interface. Although the system would consume energy, it would return energy to the grid via methane generation from composting non-edible parts of plants. It would also dramatically reduce fossil fuel use, by cutting out the need for tractors, ploughs and shipping.

A major drawback of vertical farming, however, is that the plants would require artificial light. Without it, those plants nearest the windows would be exposed to more sunlight and grow more quickly, reducing the efficiency of the system. Single-storey greenhouses have the benefit of natural overhead light: even so, many still need artificial lighting. A multi-storey facility with no natural overhead light would require far more. Generating enough light could be prohibitively expensive, unless cheap, renewable energy is available, and this appears to be rather a future aspiration than a likelihood for the near future.

One variation on vertical farming that has been developed is to grow plants in stacked trays that move on rails. Moving the trays allows the plants to get enough sunlight. This system is already in operation, and works well within a single-storey greenhouse with light reaching it from above: it is not certain, however, that it can be made to work without that overhead natural light.

Vertical farming is an attempt to address the undoubted problems that we face in producing enough food for a growing population. At the moment, though, more needs to be done to reduce the detrimental impact it would have on the environment, particularly as regards the use of energy. While it is possible that much of our food will be grown in skyscrapers in future, most experts currently believe it is far more likely that we will simply use the space available on urban rooftops.

Test 1

Questions 1–7

Complete the sentences below.

Choose **NO MORE THAN TWO WORDS** from the passage for each answer.

Write your answers in boxes 1–7 on your answer sheet.

Indoor farming

1   Some food plants, including ...., are already grown indoors.

2   Vertical farms would be located in ...., meaning that there would be less need to take them long distances to customers.

3   Vertical farms could use methane from plants and animals to produce ....

4   The consumption of .... would be cut because agricultural vehicles would be unnecessary.

5   The fact that vertical farms would need .... light is a disadvantage.

6   One form of vertical farming involves planting in .... which are not fixed.

7   The most probable development is that food will be grown on .... in towns and cities.

Questions 8–13

Do the following statements agree with the information given in Reading Passage 1?

In boxes 8–13 on your answer sheet, write

TRUE	if the statement agrees with the information
FALSE	if the statement contradicts the information
NOT GIVEN	if there is no information on this

8   Methods for predicting the Earth's population have recently changed.

9   Human beings are responsible for some of the destruction to food-producing land.

10 The crops produced in vertical farms will depend on the season.

11 Some damage to food crops is caused by climate change.

12 Fertilisers will be needed for certain crops in vertical farms.

13 Vertical farming will make plants less likely to be affected by infectious diseases.

20

READING PASSAGE 2

*You should spend about 20 minutes on **Questions 14–26**, which are based on Reading Passage 2 below.*

THE FALKIRK WHEEL

A unique engineering achievement

The Falkirk Wheel in Scotland is the world's first and only rotating boat lift. Opened in 2002, it is central to the ambitious £84.5m Millennium Link project to restore navigability across Scotland by reconnecting the historic waterways of the Forth & Clyde and Union Canals.

The major challenge of the project lay in the fact that the Forth & Clyde Canal is situated 35 metres below the level of the Union Canal. Historically, the two canals had been joined near the town of Falkirk by a sequence of 11 locks – enclosed sections of canal in which the water level could be raised or lowered – that stepped down across a distance of 1.5 km. This had been dismantled in 1933, thereby breaking the link. When the project was launched in 1994, the British Waterways authority were keen to create a dramatic twenty-first-century landmark which would not only be a fitting commemoration of the Millennium, but also a lasting symbol of the economic regeneration of the region.

Numerous ideas were submitted for the project, including concepts ranging from rolling eggs to tilting tanks, from giant see-saws to overhead monorails. The eventual winner was a plan for the huge rotating steel boat lift which was to become The Falkirk Wheel. The unique shape of the structure is claimed to have been inspired by various sources, both manmade and natural, most notably a Celtic double-headed axe, but also the vast turning propeller of a ship, the ribcage of a whale or the spine of a fish.

The various parts of The Falkirk Wheel were all constructed and assembled, like one giant toy building set, at Butterley Engineering's Steelworks in Derbyshire, some 400 km from Falkirk. A team there carefully assembled the 1,200 tonnes of steel, painstakingly fitting the pieces together to an accuracy of just 10 mm to ensure a perfect final fit. In the summer of 2001, the structure was then dismantled and transported on 35 lorries to Falkirk, before all being bolted back together again on the ground, and finally lifted into position in five large sections by crane. The Wheel would need to withstand immense and constantly changing stresses as it rotated, so to make the structure more robust, the steel sections were bolted rather than welded together. Over 45,000 bolt holes were matched with their bolts, and each bolt was hand-tightened.

The Wheel consists of two sets of opposing axe-shaped arms, attached about 25 metres apart to a fixed central spine. Two diametrically opposed water-filled 'gondolas', each with a capacity of 360,000 litres, are fitted between the ends of the arms. These gondolas always weigh the same, whether or not they are carrying boats. This is because, according to Archimedes' principle of displacement, floating objects displace their own weight in water. So when a boat enters a gondola, the amount of water leaving the gondola weighs exactly the same as the boat. This keeps the Wheel balanced and so, despite its enormous mass, it rotates through 180° in five and a half minutes while using very little power. It takes just 1.5 kilowatt-hours (5.4 MJ) of energy to rotate the Wheel – roughly the same as boiling eight small domestic kettles of water.

Boats needing to be lifted up enter the canal basin at the level of the Forth & Clyde Canal and then enter the lower gondola of the Wheel. Two hydraulic steel gates are raised, so as to seal the gondola off from the water in the canal basin. The water between the gates is then pumped out. A hydraulic clamp, which prevents the arms of the Wheel moving while the gondola is docked, is removed, allowing the Wheel to turn. In the central machine room an array of ten hydraulic motors then begins to rotate the central axle. The axle connects to the outer arms of the Wheel, which begin to rotate at a speed of 1/8 of a revolution per minute. As the wheel rotates, the gondolas are kept in the upright position by a simple gearing system. Two eight-metre-wide cogs orbit a fixed inner cog of the same width, connected by two smaller cogs travelling in the opposite direction to the outer cogs – so ensuring that the gondolas always remain level. When the gondola reaches the top, the boat passes straight onto the aqueduct situated 24 metres above the canal basin.

The remaining 11 metres of lift needed to reach the Union Canal is achieved by means of a pair of locks. The Wheel could not be constructed to elevate boats over the full 35-metre difference between the two canals, owing to the presence of the historically important Antonine Wall, which was built by the Romans in the second century AD. Boats travel under this wall via a tunnel, then through the locks, and finally on to the Union Canal.

Questions 14–19

Do the following statements agree with the information given in Reading Passage 2?

In boxes 14–19 on your answer sheet, write

> **TRUE**   *if the statement agrees with the information*
> **FALSE**   *if the statement contradicts the information*
> **NOT GIVEN**   *if there is no information on this*

14   The Falkirk Wheel has linked the Forth & Clyde Canal with the Union Canal for the first time in their history.

15   There was some opposition to the design of the Falkirk Wheel at first.

16   The Falkirk Wheel was initially put together at the location where its components were manufactured.

17   The Falkirk Wheel is the only boat lift in the world which has steel sections bolted together by hand.

18   The weight of the gondolas varies according to the size of boat being carried.

19   The construction of the Falkirk Wheel site took into account the presence of a nearby ancient monument.

Questions 20–26

Label the diagram below.

*Choose **ONE WORD** from the passage for each answer.*

Write your answers in boxes 20–26 on your answer sheet.

How a boat is lifted on the Falkirk Wheel

A pair of **20** .... are lifted in order to shut out water from canal basin

A **21** .... is taken out, enabling Wheel to rotate

26 ....
raise boat 11 m to level of Union Canal

Hydraulic motors drive **22** ....

Boat travels through tunnel beneath Roman **25** ....

Boat is raised, floating in one of Wheel's two gondolas

Boat reaches top Wheel, then moves directly onto **24** ....

A range of different-sized **23** .... ensures boat keeps upright

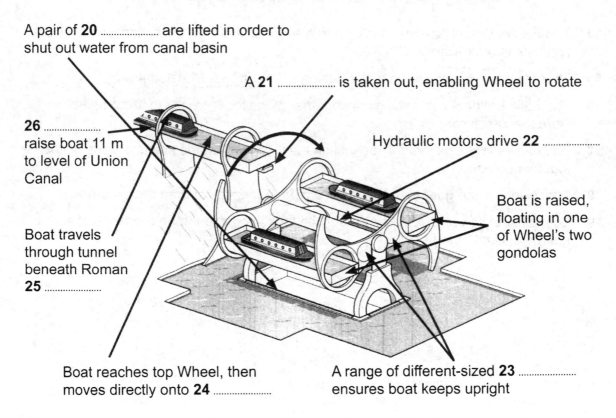

READING PASSAGE 3

*You should spend about 20 minutes on **Questions 27–40**, which are based on Reading Passage 3 below.*

Reducing the Effects of Climate Change

Mark Rowe reports on the increasingly ambitious geo-engineering projects being explored by scientists

A   Such is our dependence on fossil fuels, and such is the volume of carbon dioxide already released into the atmosphere, that many experts agree that significant global warming is now inevitable. They believe that the best we can do is keep it at a reasonable level, and at present the only serious option for doing this is cutting back on our carbon emissions. But while a few countries are making major strides in this regard, the majority are having great difficulty even stemming the rate of increase, let alone reversing it. Consequently, an increasing number of scientists are beginning to explore the alternative of geo-engineering – a term which generally refers to the intentional large-scale manipulation of the environment. According to its proponents, geo-engineering is the equivalent of a backup generator: if Plan A – reducing our dependency on fossil fuels – fails, we require a Plan B, employing grand schemes to slow down or reverse the process of global warming.

B   Geo-engineering has been shown to work, at least on a small localised scale. For decades, May Day parades in Moscow have taken place under clear blue skies, aircraft having deposited dry ice, silver iodide and cement powder to disperse clouds. Many of the schemes now suggested look to do the opposite, and reduce the amount of sunlight reaching the planet. The most eye-catching idea of all is suggested by Professor Roger Angel of the University of Arizona. His scheme would employ up to 16 trillion minute spacecraft, each weighing about one gram, to form a transparent, sunlight-refracting sunshade in an orbit 1.5 million km above the Earth. This could, argues Angel, reduce the amount of light reaching the Earth by two per cent.

C   The majority of geo-engineering projects so far carried out – which include planting forests in deserts and depositing iron in the ocean to stimulate the growth of algae – have focused on achieving a general cooling of the Earth. But some look specifically at reversing the melting at the poles, particularly the Arctic. The reasoning is that if you replenish the ice sheets and frozen waters of the high latitudes, more light will be reflected back into space, so reducing the warming of the oceans and atmosphere.

D   The concept of releasing aerosol sprays into the stratosphere above the Arctic has been proposed by several scientists. This would involve using sulphur or hydrogen sulphide aerosols so that sulphur dioxide would form clouds, which would, in turn, lead to a global dimming. The idea is modelled on historic volcanic explosions, such as that of Mount Pinatubo in the Philippines in 1991, which led to a short-term cooling of global temperatures by 0.5 °C. Scientists have also scrutinised whether it's possible to preserve the ice sheets of Greenland with reinforced high-tension cables, preventing icebergs from moving into the sea. Meanwhile in the Russian Arctic, geo-engineering plans include the planting of millions of birch trees. Whereas the region's native evergreen pines shade the snow and absorb radiation, birches would shed their leaves in winter, thus enabling radiation to be reflected by the snow. Re-routing Russian rivers to increase cold water flow to ice-forming areas could also be used to slow down warming, say some climate scientists.

E   But will such schemes ever be implemented? Generally speaking, those who are most cautious about geo-engineering are the scientists involved in the research. Angel says that his plan is 'no substitute for developing renewable energy: the only permanent solution'. And Dr Phil Rasch of the US-based Pacific Northwest National Laboratory is equally guarded about the role of geo-engineering: 'I think all of us agree that if we were to end geo-engineering on a given day, then the planet would return to its pre-engineered condition very rapidly, and probably within ten to twenty years. That's certainly something to worry about.'

F   The US National Center for Atmospheric Research has already suggested that the proposal to inject sulphur into the atmosphere might affect rainfall patterns across the tropics and the Southern Ocean. 'Geo-engineering plans to inject stratospheric aerosols or to seed clouds would act to cool the planet, and act to increase the extent of sea ice,' says Rasch. 'But all the models suggest some impact on the distribution of precipitation.'

G   'A further risk with geo-engineering projects is that you can "overshoot",' says Dr Dan Lunt, from the University of Bristol's School of Geophysical Sciences, who has studied the likely impacts of the sunshade and aerosol schemes on the climate. 'You may bring global temperatures back to pre-industrial levels, but the risk is that the poles will still be warmer than they should be and the tropics will be cooler than before industrialisation.' To avoid such a scenario, Lunt says Angel's project would have to operate at half strength; all of which reinforces his view that the best option is to avoid the need for geo-engineering altogether.

H   The main reason why geo-engineering is supported by many in the scientific community is that most researchers have little faith in the ability of politicians to agree – and then bring in – the necessary carbon cuts. Even leading conservation organisations see the value of investigating the potential of geo-engineering. According to Dr Martin Sommerkorn, climate change advisor for the World Wildlife Fund's International Arctic Programme, 'Human-induced climate change has brought humanity to a position where we shouldn't exclude thinking thoroughly about this topic and its possibilities.'

Questions 27–29

Reading Passage 3 has eight paragraphs **A–H**.

Which paragraph contains the following information?

*Write the correct letter, **A–H**, in boxes 27–29 on your answer sheet.*

27 mention of a geo-engineering project based on an earlier natural phenomenon

28 an example of a successful use of geo-engineering

29 a common definition of geo-engineering

Questions 30–36

Complete the table below.

Choose **ONE WORD** from the passage for each answer.

Write your answers in boxes 30–36 on your answer sheet.

GEO-ENGINEERING PROJECTS

Procedure	Aim
put a large number of tiny spacecraft into orbit far above Earth	to create a **30** .... that would reduce the amount of light reaching Earth
place **31** .... in the sea	to encourage **32** .... to form
release aerosol sprays into the stratosphere	to create **33** .... that would reduce the amount of light reaching Earth
fix strong **34** .... to Greenland ice sheets	to prevent icebergs moving into the sea
plant trees in Russian Arctic that would lose their leaves in winter	to allow the **35** .... to reflect radiation
change the direction of **36**	to bring more cold water into ice-forming areas

Questions 37–40

Look at the following statements (Questions 37–40) and the list of scientists below.

*Match each statement with the correct scientist, **A–D**.*

*Write the correct letter, **A–D**, in boxes 37–40 on your answer sheet.*

37 The effects of geo-engineering may not be long-lasting.

38 Geo-engineering is a topic worth exploring.

39 It may be necessary to limit the effectiveness of geo-engineering projects.

40 Research into non-fossil-based fuels cannot be replaced by geo-engineering.

List of Scientists
A Roger Angel
B Phil Rasch
C Dan Lunt
D Martin Sommerkorn

WRITING

WRITING TASK 1

You should spend about 20 minutes on this task.

> *The charts below show the percentage of water used for different purposes in six areas of the world.*
>
> *Summarise the information by selecting and reporting the main features, and make comparisons where relevant.*

Write at least 150 words.

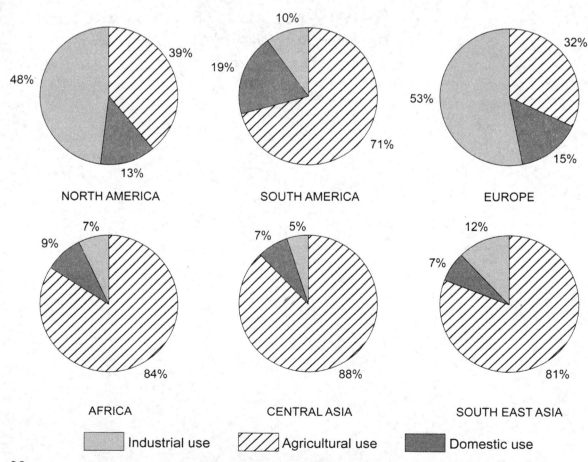

Percentage of water used for different purposes in six areas of the world

WRITING TASK 2

You should spend about 40 minutes on this task.

Write about the following topic:

> **Governments should spend money on railways rather than roads.**
>
> **To what extent do you agree or disagree with this statement?**

Give reasons for your answer and include any relevant examples from your own knowledge or experience.

Write at least 250 words.

SPEAKING

PART 1

The examiner asks the candidate about him/herself, his/her home, work or studies and other familiar topics.

EXAMPLE

Food and cooking

*   What sorts of food do you like eating most? [Why?]
*   Who normally does the cooking in your home? [Why/Why not?]
*   Do you watch cookery programmes on TV? [Why/Why not?]
*   In general, do you prefer eating out or eating at home? [Why?]

PART 2

Describe a house/apartment that someone you know lives in.
 	
You should say:
     whose house/apartment this is
     where the house/apartment is
     what it looks like inside
and explain what you like or dislike about this person's house/apartment.

You will have to talk about the topic for one to two minutes.
You have one minute to think about what you are going to say.
You can make some notes to help you if you wish.

PART 3

Discussion topics:

Different types of home

Example questions:
What kinds of home are most popular in your country? Why is this?
What do you think are the advantates of living in a house rather than an apartment?
Do you think that everyone would like to live in a larger home? Why is that?

Finding a place to live

Example questions:
How easy is it to find a place to live in your country?
Do you think it's better to rent or to buy a place to live in? Why?
Do you agree that there is a right age for young adults to stop living with their parents? Why is that?

Test 2

SECTION 1   *Questions 1–10*

Complete the notes below.

*Write **ONE WORD AND/OR A NUMBER** for each answer.*

Enquiry about joining Youth Council

Example

Name: Roger................Brown................

Age: 18

Currently staying in a **1** .... during the week

Postal address: **2** 17, ... Street, Stamford, Lincs

Postcode: **3** ....

Occupation: student and part-time job as a **4** ....

Studying **5** .... (major subject) and history (minor subject)

Hobbies: does a lot of **6** .... , and is interested in the

7 ....

On Youth Council, wants to work with young people who are

8 ....

Will come to talk to the Elections Officer next Monday at

9 .... pm

Mobile number: **10** ....

SECTION 2   *Questions 11–20*

New staff at theatre

Questions 11 and 12

*Choose **TWO** letters, **A–E**.*

Which **TWO** changes have been made so far during the refurbishment of the theatre?

    A   Some rooms now have a different use.
    B   A different type of seating has been installed.
    C   An elevator has been installed.
    D   The outside of the building has been repaired.
    E   Extra seats have been added.

Questions 13 and 14

*Choose **TWO** letters, **A–E**.*

Which **TWO** facilities does the theatre currently offer to the public?

    A   rooms for hire
    B   backstage tours
    C   hire of costumes
    D   a bookshop
    E   a café

Questions 15 and 16

*Choose **TWO** letters, **A–E**.*

Which **TWO** workshops does the theatre currently offer?

    A   sound
    B   acting
    C   making puppets
    D   make-up
    E   lighting

Questions 17–20

Label the plan below.

*Write the correct letter, **A–G**, next to Questions 17–20.*

Ground floor plan of theatre

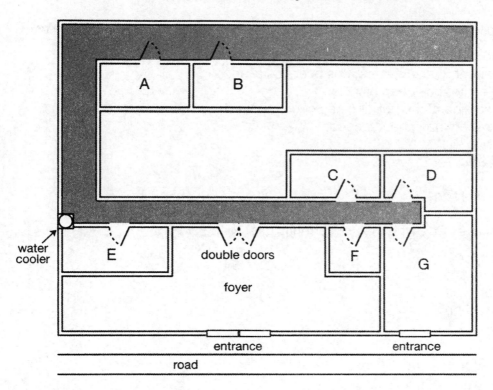

17 box office   ....

18 theatre manager's office   ....

19 lighting box   ....

20 artistic director's office   ....

SECTION 3 *Questions 21–30*

Questions 21–26

Choose the correct letter, A, B or C.

Rocky Bay field trip

21 What do the students agree should be included in their aims?

  A factors affecting where organisms live
  B the need to preserve endangered species
  C techniques for classifying different organisms

22 What equipment did they forget to take on the Field Trip?

  A string
  B a compass
  C a ruler

23 In Helen's procedure section, Colin suggests a change in

  A the order in which information is given.
  B the way the information is divided up.
  C the amount of information provided.

24 What do they say about the method they used to measure wave speed?

  A It provided accurate results.
  B It was simple to carry out.
  C It required special equipment.

25 What mistake did Helen make when first drawing the map?

  A She chose the wrong scale.
  B She stood in the wrong place.
  C She did it at the wrong time.

26 What do they decide to do next with their map?

  A scan it onto a computer
  B check it using photographs
  C add information from the internet

Questions 27 and 28

*Choose **TWO** letters, **A–E**.*

Which **TWO** problems affecting organisms in the splash zone are mentioned?

    A   lack of water
    B   strong winds
    C   lack of food
    D   high temperatures
    E   large waves

Questions 29 and 30

*Choose **TWO** letters, **A–E**.*

Which **TWO** reasons for possible error will they include in their report?

    A   inaccurate records of the habitat of organisms
    B   influence on behaviour of organisms by observer
    C   incorrect identification of some organisms
    D   making generalisations from a small sample
    E   missing some organisms when counting

SECTION 4   *Questions 31–40*

Complete the notes below.

*Write **ONE WORD ONLY** for each answer.*

DESIGNING A PUBLIC BUILDING:
THE TAYLOR CONCERT HALL

Introduction

The designer of a public building may need to consider the building's

- function

- physical and **31** .... context

- symbolic meaning

Location and concept of the Concert Hall

On the site of a disused **32** ....

Beside a **33** ....

The design is based on the concept of a mystery

Building design

It's approached by a **34** .... for pedestrians

The building is the shape of a **35** ....

One exterior wall acts as a large **36** ....

In the auditorium:

- the floor is built on huge pads made of **37** ....

- the walls are made of local wood and are **38** .... in shape

- ceiling panels and **39** .... on walls allow adjustment of acoustics

Evaluation

Some critics say the **40** .... style of the building is inappropriate

READING

READING PASSAGE 1

*You should spend about 20 minutes on **Questions 1–13**, which are based on Reading Passage 1 below.*

Raising the *Mary Rose*

How a sixteenth-century warship was recovered from the seabed

On 19 July 1545, English and French fleets were engaged in a sea battle off the coast of southern England in the area of water called the Solent, between Portsmouth and the Isle of Wight. Among the English vessels was a warship by the name of *Mary Rose*. Built in Portsmouth some 35 years earlier, she had had a long and successful fighting career, and was a favourite of King Henry VIII. Accounts of what happened to the ship vary: while witnesses agree that she was not hit by the French, some maintain that she was outdated, overladen and sailing too low in the water, others that she was mishandled by undisciplined crew. What is undisputed, however, is that the *Mary Rose* sank into the Solent that day, taking at least 500 men with her. After the battle, attempts were made to recover the ship, but these failed.

The *Mary Rose* came to rest on the seabed, lying on her starboard (right) side at an angle of approximately 60 degrees. The hull (the body of the ship) acted as a trap for the sand and mud carried by Solent currents. As a result, the starboard side filled rapidly, leaving the exposed port (left) side to be eroded by marine organisms and mechanical degradation. Because of the way the ship sank, nearly all of the starboard half survived intact. During the seventeenth and eighteenth centuries, the entire site became covered with a layer of hard grey clay, which minimised further erosion.

Then, on 16 June 1836, some fishermen in the Solent found that their equipment was caught on an underwater obstruction, which turned out to be the *Mary Rose*. Diver John Deane happened to be exploring another sunken ship nearby, and the fishermen approached him, asking him to free their gear. Deane dived down, and found the equipment caught on a timber protruding slightly from the seabed. Exploring further, he uncovered several other timbers and a bronze gun. Deane continued diving on the site intermittently until 1840, recovering several more guns, two bows, various timbers, part of a pump and various other small finds.

The *Mary Rose* then faded into obscurity for another hundred years. But in 1965, military historian and amateur diver Alexander McKee, in conjunction with the British Sub-Aqua Club, initiated a project called 'Solent Ships'. While on paper this was a plan to examine a number of known wrecks in the Solent, what McKee really hoped for was to find the *Mary Rose*. Ordinary search techniques proved unsatisfactory, so McKee entered into collaboration with Harold E. Edgerton, professor of electrical engineering at the Massachusetts Institute of Technology. In 1967, Edgerton's side-scan sonar systems revealed a large, unusually shaped object, which McKee believed was the *Mary Rose*.

Further excavations revealed stray pieces of timber and an iron gun. But the climax to the operation came when, on 5 May 1971, part of the ship's frame was uncovered. McKee and his team now knew for certain that they had found the wreck, but were as yet unaware that it also housed a treasure trove of beautifully preserved artefacts. Interest in the project grew, and in 1979, The Mary Rose Trust was formed, with Prince Charles as its President and Dr Margaret Rule its Archaeological Director. The decision whether or not to salvage the wreck was not an easy one, although an excavation in 1978 had shown that it might be possible to raise the hull. While the original aim was to raise the hull if at all feasible, the operation was not given the go-ahead until January 1982, when all the necessary information was available.

An important factor in trying to salvage the *Mary Rose* was that the remaining hull was an open shell. This led to an important decision being taken: namely to carry out the lifting operation in three very distinct stages. The hull was attached to a lifting frame via a network of bolts and lifting wires. The problem of the hull being sucked back downwards into the mud was overcome by using 12 hydraulic jacks. These raised it a few centimetres over a period of several days, as the lifting frame rose slowly up its four legs. It was only when the hull was hanging freely from the lifting frame, clear of the seabed and the suction effect of the surrounding mud, that the salvage operation progressed to the second stage. In this stage, the lifting frame was fixed to a hook attached to a crane, and the hull was lifted completely clear of the seabed and transferred underwater into the lifting cradle. This required precise positioning to locate the legs into the 'stabbing guides' of the lifting cradle. The lifting cradle was designed to fit the hull using archaeological survey drawings, and was fitted with air bags to provide additional cushioning for the hull's delicate timber framework. The third and final stage was to lift the entire structure into the air, by which time the hull was also supported from below. Finally, on 11 October 1982, millions of people around the world held their breath as the timber skeleton of the *Mary Rose* was lifted clear of the water, ready to be returned home to Portsmouth.

Questions 1–4

Do the following statements agree with the information given in Reading Passage 1?

In boxes 1–4 on your answer sheet, write

> **TRUE**　　　　*if the statement agrees with the information*
> **FALSE**　　　 *if the statement contradicts the information*
> **NOT GIVEN** *if there is no information on this*

1　There is some doubt about what caused the *Mary Rose* to sink.

2　The *Mary Rose* was the only ship to sink in the battle of 19 July 1545.

3　Most of one side of the *Mary Rose* lay undamaged under the sea.

4　Alexander McKee knew that the wreck would contain many valuable historical objects.

Questions 5–8

Look at the following statements (Questions 5–8) and the list of dates below.

*Match each statement with the correct date, **A–G**.*

*Write the correct letter, **A–G**, in boxes 5–8 on your answer sheet.*

5　A search for the *Mary Rose* was launched.

6　One person's exploration of the *Mary Rose* site stopped.

7　It was agreed that the hull of the *Mary Rose* should be raised.

8　The site of the *Mary Rose* was found by chance.

List of Dates			
A	1836	**E**	1971
B	1840	**F**	1979
C	1965	**G**	1982
D	1967		

Questions 9–13

Label the diagram below.

Choose **NO MORE THAN TWO WORDS** from the passage for each answer.

Write your answers in boxes 9–13 on your answer sheet.

Raising the hull of the *Mary Rose*: Stages one and two

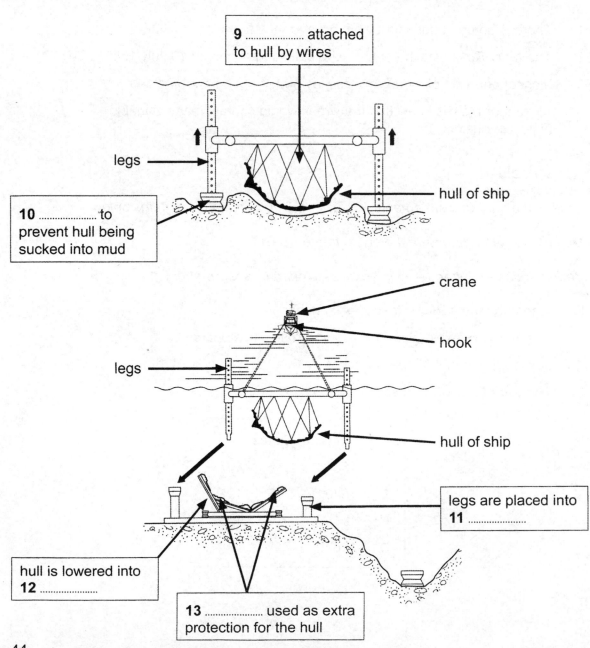

9 .... attached to hull by wires

legs

10 .... to prevent hull being sucked into mud

hull of ship

crane

hook

legs

hull of ship

legs are placed into 11 ....

hull is lowered into 12 ....

13 .... used as extra protection for the hull

READING PASSAGE 2

*You should spend about 20 minutes on **Questions 14–26**, which are based on Reading Passage 2 on the following pages.*

Questions 14–20

Reading Passage 2 has seven paragraphs, **A–G**.

Choose the correct heading for each paragraph from the list of headings below.

*Write the correct number, **i–ix**, in boxes 14–20 on your answer sheet.*

	List of Headings
i	Evidence of innovative environment management practices
ii	An undisputed answer to a question about the moai
iii	The future of the moai statues
iv	A theory which supports a local belief
v	The future of Easter Island
vi	Two opposing views about the Rapanui people
vii	Destruction outside the inhabitants' control
viii	How the statues made a situation worse
ix	Diminishing food resources

14 Paragraph **A**

15 Paragraph **B**

16 Paragraph **C**

17 Paragraph **D**

18 Paragraph **E**

19 Paragraph **F**

20 Paragraph **G**

What destroyed the civilisation of Easter Island?

A   Easter Island, or Rapu Nui as it is known locally, is home to several hundred ancient human statues – the *moai*. After this remote Pacific island was settled by the Polynesians, it remained isolated for centuries. All the energy and resources that went into the moai – some of which are ten metres tall and weigh over 7,000 kilos – came from the island itself. Yet when Dutch explorers landed in 1722, they met a Stone Age culture. The moai were carved with stone tools, then transported for many kilometres, without the use of animals or wheels, to massive stone platforms. The identity of the moai builders was in doubt until well into the twentieth century. Thor Heyerdahl, the Norwegian ethnographer and adventurer, thought the statues had been created by pre-Inca peoples from Peru. Bestselling Swiss author Erich von Däniken believed they were built by stranded extraterrestrials. Modern science – linguistic, archaeological and genetic evidence – has definitively proved the moai builders were Polynesians, but not how they moved their creations. Local folklore maintains that the statues walked, while researchers have tended to assume the ancestors dragged the statues somehow, using ropes and logs.

B   When the Europeans arrived, Rapa Nui was grassland, with only a few scrawny trees. In the 1970s and 1980s, though, researchers found pollen preserved in lake sediments, which proved the island had been covered in lush palm forests for thousands of years. Only after the Polynesians arrived did those forests disappear. US scientist Jared Diamond believes that the Rapanui people – descendants of Polynesian settlers – wrecked their own environment. They had unfortunately settled on an extremely fragile island – dry, cool, and too remote to be properly fertilised by windblown volcanic ash. When the islanders cleared the forests for firewood and farming, the forests didn't grow back. As trees became scarce and they could no longer construct wooden canoes for fishing, they ate birds. Soil erosion decreased their crop yields. Before Europeans arrived, the Rapanui had descended into civil war and cannibalism, he maintains. The collapse of their isolated civilisation, Diamond writes, is a 'worst-case scenario for what may lie ahead of us in our own future'.

C   The moai, he thinks, accelerated the self-destruction. Diamond interprets them as power displays by rival chieftains who, trapped on a remote little island, lacked other ways of asserting their dominance. They competed by building ever bigger figures. Diamond thinks they laid the moai on wooden sledges, hauled over log rails, but that required both a lot of wood and a lot of people. To feed the people, even more land had to be cleared. When the wood was gone and civil war began, the islanders began toppling the moai. By the nineteenth century none were standing.

D   Archaeologists Terry Hunt of the University of Hawaii and Carl Lipo of California State University agree that Easter Island lost its lush forests and that it was an 'ecological catastrophe' – but they believe the islanders themselves weren't to blame. And the moai certainly weren't. Archaeological excavations indicate that the Rapanui went to heroic efforts to protect the resources of their wind-lashed, infertile fields. They built thousands of circular stone windbreaks and gardened inside them, and used broken volcanic rocks to keep the soil moist. In short, Hunt and Lipo argue, the prehistoric Rapanui were pioneers of sustainable farming.

E   Hunt and Lipo contend that moai-building was an activity that helped keep the peace between islanders. They also believe that moving the moai required few people and no wood, because they were walked upright. On that issue, Hunt and Lipo say, archaeological evidence backs up Rapanui folklore. Recent experiments indicate that as few as 18 people could, with three strong ropes and a bit of practice, easily manoeuvre a 1,000 kg moai replica a few hundred metres. The figures' fat bellies tilted them forward, and a D-shaped base allowed handlers to roll and rock them side to side.

F   Moreover, Hunt and Lipo are convinced that the settlers were not wholly responsible for the loss of the island's trees. Archaeological finds of nuts from the extinct Easter Island palm show tiny grooves, made by the teeth of Polynesian rats. The rats arrived along with the settlers, and in just a few years, Hunt and Lipo calculate, they would have overrun the island. They would have prevented the reseeding of the slow-growing palm trees and thereby doomed Rapa Nui's forest, even without the settlers' campaign of deforestation. No doubt the rats ate birds' eggs too. Hunt and Lipo also see no evidence that Rapanui civilisation collapsed when the palm forest did. They think its population grew rapidly and then remained more or less stable until the arrival of the Europeans, who introduced deadly diseases to which islanders had no immunity. Then in the nineteenth century slave traders decimated the population, which shrivelled to 111 people by 1877.

G   Hunt and Lipo's vision, therefore, is one of an island populated by peaceful and ingenious moai builders and careful stewards of the land, rather than by reckless destroyers ruining their own environment and society. 'Rather than a case of abject failure, Rapu Nui is an unlikely story of success', they claim. Whichever is the case, there are surely some valuable lessons which the world at large can learn from the story of Rapa Nui.

Questions 21–24

Complete the summary below.

Choose **ONE WORD ONLY** from the passage for each answer.

Write your answers in boxes 21–24 on your answer sheet.

Jared Diamond's View

Diamond believes that the Polynesian settlers on Rapa Nui destroyed its forests, cutting down its trees for fuel and clearing land for **21** .... Twentieth-century discoveries of pollen prove that Rapu Nui had once been covered in palm forests, which had turned into grassland by the time the Europeans arrived on the island. When the islanders were no longer able to build the **22** .... they needed to go fishing, they began using the island's **23** .... as a food source, according to Diamond. Diamond also claims that the moai were built to show the power of the island's chieftains, and that the methods of transporting the statues needed not only a great number of people, but also a great deal of **24** ....

Questions 25 and 26

Choose **TWO** letters, **A–E**.

Write the correct letters in boxes 25 and 26 on your answer sheet.

On what points do Hunt and Lipo disagree with Diamond?

    A   the period when the moai were created
    B   how the moai were transported
    C   the impact of the moai on Rapanui society
    D   how the moai were carved
    E   the origins of the people who made the moai

READING PASSAGE 3

*You should spend about 20 minutes on **Questions 27–40**, which are based on Reading Passage 3 below.*

Neuroaesthetics

An emerging discipline called neuroaesthetics is seeking to bring scientific objectivity to the study of art, and has already given us a better understanding of many masterpieces. The blurred imagery of Impressionist paintings seems to stimulate the brain's amygdala, for instance. Since the amygdala plays a crucial role in our feelings, that finding might explain why many people find these pieces so moving.

Could the same approach also shed light on abstract twentieth-century pieces, from Mondrian's geometrical blocks of colour, to Pollock's seemingly haphazard arrangements of splashed paint on canvas? Sceptics believe that people claim to like such works simply because they are famous. We certainly do have an inclination to follow the crowd. When asked to make simple perceptual decisions such as matching a shape to its rotated image, for example, people often choose a definitively wrong answer if they see others doing the same. It is easy to imagine that this mentality would have even more impact on a fuzzy concept like art appreciation, where there is no right or wrong answer.

Angelina Hawley-Dolan, of Boston College, Massachusetts, responded to this debate by asking volunteers to view pairs of paintings – either the creations of famous abstract artists or the doodles of infants, chimps and elephants. They then had to judge which they preferred. A third of the paintings were given no captions, while many were labelled incorrectly – volunteers might think they were viewing a chimp's messy brushstrokes when they were actually seeing an acclaimed masterpiece. In each set of trials, volunteers generally preferred the work of renowned artists, even when they believed it was by an animal or a child. It seems that the viewer can sense the artist's vision in paintings, even if they can't explain why.

Robert Pepperell, an artist based at Cardiff University, creates ambiguous works that are neither entirely abstract nor clearly representational. In one study, Pepperell and his collaborators asked volunteers to decide how 'powerful' they considered an artwork to be, and whether they saw anything familiar in the piece. The longer they took to answer these questions, the more highly they rated the piece under scrutiny, and the greater their neural activity. It would seem that the brain sees these images as puzzles, and the harder it is to decipher the meaning, the more rewarding is the moment of recognition.

And what about artists such as Mondrian, whose paintings consist exclusively of horizontal and vertical lines encasing blocks of colour? Mondrian's works are deceptively simple, but eye-tracking studies confirm that they are meticulously composed, and that simply rotating a piece radically changes the way we view it. With the originals, volunteers' eyes tended to stay longer on certain places in the image, but with the altered versions they would flit across a piece more rapidly. As a result, the volunteers considered the altered versions less pleasurable when they later rated the work.

In a similar study, Oshin Vartanian of Toronto University asked volunteers to compare original paintings with ones which he had altered by moving objects around within the frame. He found that almost everyone preferred the original, whether it was a Van Gogh still life or an abstract by Miró. Vartanian also found that changing the composition of the paintings reduced activation in those brain areas linked with meaning and interpretation.

In another experiment, Alex Forsythe of the University of Liverpool analysed the visual intricacy of different pieces of art, and her results suggest that many artists use a key level of detail to please the brain. Too little and the work is boring, but too much results in a kind of 'perceptual overload', according to Forsythe. What's more, appealing pieces both abstract and representational, show signs of 'fractals' – repeated motifs recurring in different scales. Fractals are common throughout nature, for example in the shapes of mountain peaks or the branches of trees. It is possible that our visual system, which evolved in the great outdoors, finds it easier to process such patterns.

It is also intriguing that the brain appears to process movement when we see a handwritten letter, as if we are replaying the writer's moment of creation. This has led some to wonder whether Pollock's works feel so dynamic because the brain reconstructs the energetic actions the artist used as he painted. This may be down to our brain's 'mirror neurons', which are known to mimic others' actions. The hypothesis will need to be thoroughly tested, however. It might even be the case that we could use neuroaesthetic studies to understand the longevity of some pieces of artwork. While the fashions of the time might shape what is currently popular, works that are best adapted to our visual system may be the most likely to linger once the trends of previous generations have been forgotten.

It's still early days for the field of neuroaesthetics – and these studies are probably only a taste of what is to come. It would, however, be foolish to reduce art appreciation to a set of scientific laws. We shouldn't underestimate the importance of the style of a particular artist, their place in history and the artistic environment of their time. Abstract art offers both a challenge and the freedom to play with different interpretations. In some ways, it's not so different to science, where we are constantly looking for systems and decoding meaning so that we can view and appreciate the world in a new way.

Questions 27–30

*Choose the correct letter, **A**, **B**, **C** or **D**.*

Write the correct letter in boxes 27–30 on your answer sheet.

27 In the second paragraph, the writer refers to a shape-matching test in order to illustrate

    A   the subjective nature of art appreciation.
    B   the reliance of modern art on abstract forms.
    C   our tendency to be influenced by the opinions of others.
    D   a common problem encountered when processing visual data.

28 Angelina Hawley-Dolan's findings indicate that people

    A   mostly favour works of art which they know well.
    B   hold fixed ideas about what makes a good work of art.
    C   are often misled by their initial expectations of a work of art.
    D   have the ability to perceive the intention behind works of art.

29 Results of studies involving Robert Pepperell's pieces suggest that people

    A   can appreciate a painting without fully understanding it.
    B   find it satisfying to work out what a painting represents.
    C   vary widely in the time they spend looking at paintings.
    D   generally prefer representational art to abstract art.

30 What do the experiments described in the fifth paragraph suggest about the paintings of Mondrian?

    A   They are more carefully put together than they appear.
    B   They can be interpreted in a number of different ways.
    C   They challenge our assumptions about shape and colour.
    D   They are easier to appreciate than many other abstract works.

Questions 31–33

*Complete the summary using the list of words, **A–H**, below.*

*Write the correct letters, **A–H**, in boxes 31–33 on your answer sheet.*

Art and the Brain

The discipline of neuroaesthetics aims to bring scientific objectivity to the study of art. Neurological studies of the brain, for example, demonstrate the impact which Impressionist paintings have on our **31** .... Alex Forsythe of the University of Liverpool believes many artists give their works the precise degree of **32** .... which most appeals to the viewer's brain. She also observes that pleasing works of art often contain certain repeated **33** .... which occur frequently in the natural world.

A	interpretation	**B**	complexity	**C**	emotions
D	movements	**E**	skill	**F**	layout
G	concern	**H**	images		

Questions 34–39

Do the following statements agree with the views of the writer in Reading Passage 3?

In boxes 34–39 on your answer sheet, write

> **YES**　　　　*if the statement agrees with the views of the writer*
> **NO**　　　　 *if the statement contradicts the views of the writer*
> **NOT GIVEN** *if there is no information on this*

34　Forsythe's findings contradicted previous beliefs on the function of 'fractals' in art.

35　Certain ideas regarding the link between 'mirror neurons' and art appreciation require further verification.

36　People's taste in paintings depends entirely on the current artistic trends of the period.

37　Scientists should seek to define the precise rules which govern people's reactions to works of art.

38　Art appreciation should always involve taking into consideration the cultural context in which an artist worked.

39　It is easier to find meaning in the field of science than in that of art.

Question 40

*Choose the correct letter, **A**, **B**, **C** or **D**.*

Write the correct letter in box 40 on your answer sheet.

40　What would be the most appropriate subtitle for the article?

　　A　Some scientific insights into how the brain responds to abstract art
　　B　Recent studies focusing on the neural activity of abstract artists
　　C　A comparison of the neurological bases of abstract and representational art
　　D　How brain research has altered public opinion about abstract art

WRITING

WRITING TASK 1

You should spend about 20 minutes on this task.

The charts below show the proportions of British students at one university in England who were able to speak other languages in addition to English, in 2000 and 2010.

Summarise the information by selecting and reporting the main features, and make comparisons where relevant.

Write at least 150 words.

% of British Students able to speak languages other than English, 2000

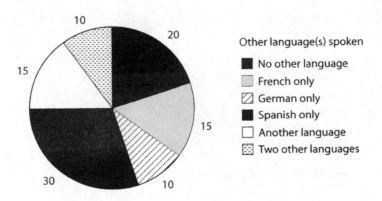

% of British Students able to speak languages other than English, 2010

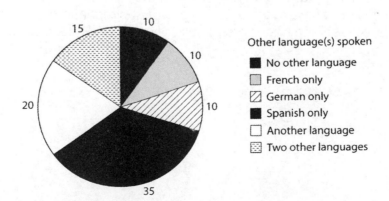

WRITING TASK 2

You should spend about 40 minutes on this task.

Write about the following topic:

Some people claim that not enough of the waste from homes is recycled. They say that the only way to increase recycling is for governments to make it a legal requirement.

To what extent do you think laws are needed to make people recycle more of their waste?

Give reasons for your answer and include any relevant examples from your own knowledge or experience.

Write at least 250 words.

SPEAKING

PART 1

The examiner asks the candidate about him/herself, his/her home, work or studies and other familiar topics.

EXAMPLE

Friends

- How often do you go out with friends? [Why/Why not?]
- Tell me about your best friend at school.
- How friendly are you with your neighbours? [Why/Why not?]
- Which is more important to you, friends or family? [Why?]

PART 2

Describe a writer you would like to meet.
You should say:
who the writer is
what you know about this writer already
what you would like to find out about him/her
and explain why you would like to meet this writer.

You will have to talk about the topic for one to two minutes. You have one minute to think about what you are going to say. You can make some notes to help you if you wish.

PART 3

Discussion topics:

Reading and children

Example questions:
What kinds of book are most popular with children in your country? Why do you think that is?
Why do you think some children do not read books very often?
How do you think children can be encouraged to read more?

Reading for different purposes

Example questions:
Are there any occasions when reading at speed is a useful skill to have? What are they?
Are there any jobs where people need to read a lot? What are they?
Do you think that reading novels is more interesting than reading factual books? Why is that?

Test 3

SECTION 1   *Questions 1–10*

Questions 1–6

*Choose the correct letter, **A**, **B** or **C**.*

Free activities in the Burnham area

Example

The caller wants to find out about events on

  A   27 June.
  B   28 June.
  ©   29 June.

---

1 The 'Family Welcome' event in the art gallery begins at

  A   10 am.
  B   10.30 am.
  C   2 pm.

2 The film that is now shown in the 'Family Welcome' event is about

  A   sculpture.
  B   painting.
  C   ceramics.

3 When do most of the free concerts take place?

  A   in the morning
  B   at lunchtime
  C   in the evening

4 Where will the 4 pm concert of Latin American music take place?

  A   in a museum
  B   in a theatre
  C   in a library

5 The boat race begins at

  A   Summer Pool.
  B   Charlesworth Bridge.
  C   Offord Marina.

6 One of the boat race teams

  A   won a regional competition earlier this year.
  B   has represented the region in a national competition.
  C   has won several regional competitions.

Questions 7–10

Complete the sentences below.

Write **ONE WORD ONLY** for each answer.

Paxton Nature Reserve

7   Paxton is a good place for seeing rare .... all year round.

8   This is a particularly good time for seeing certain unusual ....

9   Visitors will be able to learn about .... and then collect some.

10   Part of the .... has been made suitable for swimming.

SECTION 2   *Questions 11–20*

Questions 11–15

*Choose the correct letter, **A**, **B** or **C**.*

Changes in Barford over the last 50 years

11   In Shona's opinion, why do fewer people use buses in Barford these days?

   A   The buses are old and uncomfortable.
   B   Fares have gone up too much.
   C   There are not so many bus routes.

12   What change in the road network is known to have benefited the town most?

   A   the construction of a bypass
   B   the development of cycle paths
   C   the banning of cars from certain streets

13   What is the problem affecting shopping in the town centre?

   A   lack of parking spaces
   B   lack of major retailers
   C   lack of restaurants and cafés

14   What does Shona say about medical facilities in Barford?

   A   There is no hospital.
   B   New medical practices are planned.
   C   The number of dentists is too low.

15   The largest number of people are employed in

   A   manufacturing.
   B   services.
   C   education.

Questions 16–20

What is planned for each of the following facilities?

*Choose **FIVE** answers from the box and write the correct letter, **A–G**, next to Questions 16–20.*

Plans
A   It will move to a new location.
B   It will have its opening hours extended.
C   It will be refurbished.
D   It will be used for a different purpose.
E   It will have its opening hours reduced.
F   It will have new management.
G   It will be expanded.

Facilities

16 railway station car park ....

17 cinema ....

18 indoor market ....

19 library ....

20 nature reserve ....

SECTION 3   *Questions 21–30*

Questions 21–26

Complete the table below.

*Write **ONE WORD ONLY** for each answer.*

Subject of drawing	Change to be made
A **21** .... surrounded by trees	Add Malcolm and a **22** .... noticing him
People who are **23** .... outside the forest	Add Malcolm sitting on a tree trunk and **24** ....
Ice-skaters on **25** .... covered with ice	Add a **26** .... for each person

Questions 27–30

Who is going to write each of the following parts of the report?

*Write the correct letter, **A–D**, next to Questions 27–30.*

A	Helen only
B	Jeremy only
C	both Helen and Jeremy
D	neither Helen nor Jeremy

Parts of the report

27 how they planned the project   ....

28 how they had ideas for their stories   ....

29 an interpretation of their stories   ....

30 comments on the illustrations   ....

SECTION 4   *Questions 31–40*

Complete the notes below.

Write **ONE WORD ONLY** *for each answer.*

ETHNOGRAPHY IN BUSINESS

Ethnography: research which explores human cultures

It can be used in business:

- to investigate customer needs and **31** ....

- to help companies develop new designs

Examples of ethnographic research in business

Kitchen equipment

- Researchers found that cooks could not easily see the **32** ....
  in measuring cups.

Cell phones

- In Uganda, customers paid to use the cell phones of entrepreneurs.

- These customers wanted to check the **33** .... used.

Computer companies

- There was a need to develop **34** .... to improve communication
  between system administrators and colleagues.

Hospitals

- Nurses needed to access information about **35** .... in different
  parts of the hospital.

Airlines

- Respondents recorded information about their **36** .... while
  travelling.

Principles of ethnographic research in business

- The researcher does not start off with a hypothesis.

- Participants may be selected by criteria such as age, **37** .... or product used.

- The participants must feel **38** .... about taking part in the research.

- There is usually direct **39** .... of the participants.

- The interview is guided by the participant.

- A lot of time is needed for the **40** .... of the data.

- Researchers look for a meaningful pattern in the data.

READING PASSAGE 1

*You should spend about 20 minutes on **Questions 1–13**, which are based on Reading Passage 1 below.*

THE STORY OF SILK

The history of the world's most luxurious fabric, from ancient China to the present day

Silk is a fine, smooth material produced from the cocoons – soft protective shells – that are made by mulberry silkworms (insect larvae). Legend has it that it was Lei Tzu, wife of the Yellow Emperor, ruler of China in about 3000 BC, who discovered silkworms. One account of the story goes that as she was taking a walk in her husband's gardens, she discovered that silkworms were responsible for the destruction of several mulberry trees. She collected a number of cocoons and sat down to have a rest. It just so happened that while she was sipping some tea, one of the cocoons that she had collected landed in the hot tea and started to unravel into a fine thread. Lei Tzu found that she could wind this thread around her fingers. Subsequently, she persuaded her husband to allow her to rear silkworms on a grove of mulberry trees. She also devised a special reel to draw the fibres from the cocoon into a single thread so that they would be strong enough to be woven into fabric. While it is unknown just how much of this is true, it is certainly known that silk cultivation has existed in China for several millennia.

Originally, silkworm farming was solely restricted to women, and it was they who were responsible for the growing, harvesting and weaving. Silk quickly grew into a symbol of status, and originally, only royalty were entitled to have clothes made of silk. The rules were gradually relaxed over the years until finally during the Qing Dynasty (1644–1911 AD), even peasants, the lowest caste, were also entitled to wear silk. Sometime during the Han Dynasty (206 BC–220 AD), silk was so prized that it was also used as a unit of currency. Government officials were paid their salary in silk, and farmers paid their taxes in grain and silk. Silk was also used as diplomatic gifts by the emperor. Fishing lines, bowstrings, musical instruments and paper were all made using silk. The earliest indication of silk paper being used was discovered in the tomb of a noble who is estimated to have died around 168 AD.

Demand for this exotic fabric eventually created the lucrative trade route now known as the Silk Road, taking silk westward and bringing gold, silver and wool to the East. It was named the Silk Road after its most precious commodity, which was considered to be worth more than gold. The Silk Road stretched over 6,000 kilometres from Eastern China to the Mediterranean Sea, following the Great Wall of China, climbing the Pamir mountain range, crossing modern-day Afghanistan and going on to the Middle East, with a major trading market in Damascus. From there, the merchandise was shipped across the Mediterranean Sea. Few merchants travelled the entire route; goods were handled mostly by a series of middlemen.

With the mulberry silkworm being native to China, the country was the world's sole producer of silk for many hundreds of years. The secret of silk-making eventually reached the rest of the world via the Byzantine Empire, which ruled over the Mediterranean region of southern Europe, North Africa and the Middle East during the period 330–1453 AD. According to another legend, monks working for the Byzantine emperor Justinian smuggled silkworm eggs to Constantinople (Istanbul in modern-day Turkey) in 550 AD, concealed inside hollow bamboo walking canes. The Byzantines were as secretive as the Chinese, however, and for many centuries the weaving and trading of silk fabric was a strict imperial monopoly. Then in the seventh century, the Arabs conquered Persia, capturing their magnificent silks in the process. Silk production thus spread through Africa, Sicily and Spain as the Arabs swept through these lands. Andalusia in southern Spain was Europe's main silk-producing centre in the tenth century. By the thirteenth century, however, Italy had become Europe's leader in silk production and export. Venetian merchants traded extensively in silk and encouraged silk growers to settle in Italy. Even now, silk processed in the province of Como in northern Italy enjoys an esteemed reputation.

The nineteenth century and industrialisation saw the downfall of the European silk industry. Cheaper Japanese silk, trade in which was greatly facilitated by the opening of the Suez Canal, was one of the many factors driving the trend. Then in the twentieth century, new manmade fibres, such as nylon, started to be used in what had traditionally been silk products, such as stockings and parachutes. The two world wars, which interrupted the supply of raw material from Japan, also stifled the European silk industry. After the Second World War, Japan's silk production was restored, with improved production and quality of raw silk. Japan was to remain the world's biggest producer of raw silk, and practically the only major exporter of raw silk, until the 1970s. However, in more recent decades, China has gradually recaptured its position as the world's biggest producer and exporter of raw silk and silk yarn. Today, around 125,000 metric tons of silk are produced in the world, and almost two thirds of that production takes place in China.

Questions 1–9

Complete the notes below.

*Choose **ONE WORD ONLY** from the passage for each answer.*

Write your answers in boxes 1–9 on your answer sheet.

THE STORY OF SILK

Early silk production in China

- Around 3000 BC, according to legend:
    - silkworm cocoon fell into emperor's wife's **1** ....
    - emperor's wife invented a **2** .... to pull out silk fibres
- Only **3** .... were allowed to produce silk
- Only **4** .... were allowed to wear silk
- Silk used as a form of **5** ....
    - e.g. farmers' taxes consisted partly of silk
- Silk used for many purposes
    - e.g. evidence found of **6** .... made from silk around 168 AD

Silk reaches rest of world

- Merchants use Silk Road to take silk westward and bring back **7** .... and precious metals
- 550 AD: **8** .... hide silkworm eggs in canes and take them to Constantinople
- Silk production spreads across Middle East and Europe
- 20th century: **9** .... and other manmade fibres cause decline in silk production

Do the following statements agree with the information in Reading Passage 1?

In boxes 10–13 on your answer sheet, write

> **TRUE**   *if the statement agrees with the information*
> **FALSE**   *if the statement contradicts the information*
> **NOT GIVEN**   *if there is no information on this*

10   Gold was the most valuable material transported along the Silk Road.

11   Most tradesmen only went along certain sections of the Silk Road.

12   The Byzantines spread the practice of silk production across the West.

13   Silk yarn makes up the majority of silk currently exported from China.

READING PASSAGE 2

*You should spend about 20 minutes on **Questions 14–26**, which are based on Reading Passage 2 below.*

Great Migrations

Animal migration, however it is defined, is far more than just the movement of animals. It can loosely be described as travel that takes place at regular intervals – often in an annual cycle – that may involve many members of a species, and is rewarded only after a long journey. It suggests inherited instinct. The biologist Hugh Dingle has identified five characteristics that apply, in varying degrees and combinations, to all migrations. They are prolonged movements that carry animals outside familiar habitats; they tend to be linear, not zigzaggy; they involve special behaviours concerning preparation (such as overfeeding) and arrival; they demand special allocations of energy. And one more: migrating animals maintain an intense attentiveness to the greater mission, which keeps them undistracted by temptations and undeterred by challenges that would turn other animals aside.

An arctic tern, on its 20,000 km flight from the extreme south of South America to the Arctic circle, will take no notice of a nice smelly herring offered from a bird-watcher's boat along the way. While local gulls will dive voraciously for such handouts, the tern flies on. Why? The arctic tern resists distraction because it is driven at that moment by an instinctive sense of something we humans find admirable: larger purpose. In other words, it is determined to reach its destination. The bird senses that it can eat, rest and mate later. Right now it is totally focused on the journey; its undivided intent is arrival.

Reaching some gravelly coastline in the Arctic, upon which other arctic terns have converged, will serve its larger purpose as shaped by evolution: finding a place, a time, and a set of circumstances in which it can successfully hatch and rear offspring.

But migration is a complex issue, and biologists define it differently, depending in part on what sorts of animals they study. Joel Berger, of the University of Montana, who works on the American pronghorn and other large terrestrial mammals, prefers what he calls a simple, practical definition suited to his beasts: 'movements from a seasonal home area away to another home area and back again'. Generally the reason for such seasonal back-and-forth movement is to seek resources that aren't available within a single area year-round.

But daily vertical movements by zooplankton in the ocean – upward by night to seek food, downward by day to escape predators – can also be considered migration. So can the movement of aphids when, having depleted the young leaves on one food plant, their offspring then fly onward to a different host plant, with no one aphid ever returning to where it started.

Dingle is an evolutionary biologist who studies insects. His definition is more intricate than Berger's, citing those five features that distinguish migration from other forms of movement. They allow for the fact that, for example, aphids will become sensitive to blue light (from the sky) when it's time for takeoff on their big journey, and sensitive to yellow light (reflected from tender young leaves) when it's appropriate to land. Birds will fatten themselves with heavy feeding in advance of a long migrational flight. The value of his definition, Dingle argues, is that it focuses attention on what the phenomenon of wildebeest migration shares with the phenomenon of the aphids, and therefore helps guide researchers towards understanding how evolution has produced them all.

Human behaviour, however, is having a detrimental impact on animal migration. The pronghorn, which resembles an antelope, though they are unrelated, is the fastest land mammal of the New World. One population, which spends the summer in the mountainous Grand Teton National Park of the western USA, follows a narrow route from its summer range in the mountains, across a river, and down onto the plains. Here they wait out the frozen months, feeding mainly on sagebrush blown clear of snow. These pronghorn are notable for the invariance of their migration route and the severity of its constriction at three bottlenecks. If they can't pass through each of the three during their spring migration, they can't reach their bounty of summer grazing; if they can't

pass through again in autumn, escaping south onto those windblown plains, they are likely to die trying to overwinter in the deep snow. Pronghorn, dependent on distance vision and speed to keep safe from predators, traverse high, open shoulders of land, where they can see and run. At one of the bottlenecks, forested hills rise to form a V, leaving a corridor of open ground only about 150 metres wide, filled with private homes. Increasing development is leading toward a crisis for the pronghorn, threatening to choke off their passageway.

Conservation scientists, along with some biologists and land managers within the USA's National Park Service and other agencies, are now working to preserve migrational behaviours, not just species and habitats. A National Forest has recognised the path of the pronghorn, much of which passes across its land, as a protected migration corridor. But neither the Forest Service nor the Park Service can control what happens on private land at a bottleneck. And with certain other migrating species, the challenge is complicated further – by vastly greater distances traversed, more jurisdictions, more borders, more dangers along the way. We will require wisdom and resoluteness to ensure that migrating species can continue their journeying a while longer.

Questions 14–18

Do the following statements agree with the information given in Reading Passage 2?

In boxes 14–18 on your answer sheet, write

> **TRUE**   *if the statement agrees with the information*
> **FALSE**   *if the statement contradicts the information*
> **NOT GIVEN** *if there is no information on this*

14 Local gulls and migrating arctic terns behave in the same way when offered food.

15 Experts' definitions of migration tend to vary according to their area of study.

16 Very few experts agree that the movement of aphids can be considered migration.

17 Aphids' journeys are affected by changes in the light that they perceive.

18 Dingle's aim is to distinguish between the migratory behaviours of different species.

Questions 19–22

Complete each sentence with the correct ending, **A–G**, below.

Write the correct letter, **A–G**, in boxes 19–22 on your answer sheet.

19 According to Dingle, migratory routes are likely to

20 To prepare for migration, animals are likely to

21 During migration, animals are unlikely to

22 Arctic terns illustrate migrating animals' ability to

A	be discouraged by difficulties.
B	travel on open land where they can look out for predators.
C	eat more than they need for immediate purposes.
D	be repeated daily.
E	ignore distractions.
F	be governed by the availability of water.
G	follow a straight line.

Questions 23–26

Complete the summary below.

Choose **ONE WORD ONLY** from the passage for each answer.

Write your answers in boxes 23–26 on your answer sheet.

The migration of pronghorns

Pronghorns rely on their eyesight and **23** .... to avoid predators. One particular population's summer habitat is a national park, and their winter home is on the **24** .... , where they go to avoid the danger presented by the snow at that time of year. However, their route between these two areas contains three **25** .... One problem is the construction of new homes in a narrow **26**.................... of land on the pronghorns' route.

READING PASSAGE 3

*You should spend about 20 minutes on **Questions 27–40**, which are based on Reading Passage 3 below.*

Preface to 'How the other half thinks: Adventures in mathematical reasoning'

A   Occasionally, in some difficult musical compositions, there are beautiful, but easy parts – parts so simple a beginner could play them. So it is with mathematics as well. There are some discoveries in advanced mathematics that do not depend on specialized knowledge, not even on algebra, geometry, or trigonometry. Instead they may involve, at most, a little arithmetic, such as 'the sum of two odd numbers is even', and common sense. Each of the eight chapters in this book illustrates this phenomenon. Anyone can understand every step in the reasoning.

The thinking in each chapter uses at most only elementary arithmetic, and sometimes not even that. Thus all readers will have the chance to participate in a mathematical experience, to appreciate the beauty of mathematics, and to become familiar with its logical, yet intuitive, style of thinking.

B   One of my purposes in writing this book is to give readers who haven't had the opportunity to see and enjoy real mathematics the chance to appreciate the mathematical way of thinking. I want to reveal not only some of the fascinating discoveries, but, more importantly, the reasoning behind them.

In that respect, this book differs from most books on mathematics written for the general public. Some present the lives of colorful mathematicians. Others describe important applications of mathematics. Yet others go into mathematical procedures, but assume that the reader is adept in using algebra.

C   I hope this book will help bridge that notorious gap that separates the two cultures: the humanities and the sciences, or should I say the right brain (intuitive) and the left brain (analytical, numerical). As the chapters will illustrate, mathematics is not restricted to the analytical and numerical; intuition plays a significant role. The alleged gap can be narrowed or completely overcome by anyone, in part because each of us is far from using the full capacity of either side of the brain. To illustrate our human potential, I cite a structural engineer who is an artist, an electrical engineer who is an opera singer, an opera singer who published mathematical research, and a mathematician who publishes short stories.

D   Other scientists have written books to explain their fields to non-scientists, but have necessarily had to omit the mathematics, although it provides the foundation of their theories. The reader must remain a tantalized spectator rather than an involved participant, since the appropriate language for describing the details in much of science is mathematics, whether the subject is expanding universe, subatomic particles, or chromosomes. Though the broad outline of a scientific theory can be sketched intuitively, when a part of the physical universe is finally understood, its description often looks like a page in a mathematics text.

E Still, the non-mathematical reader can go far in understanding mathematical reasoning. This book presents the details that illustrate the mathematical style of thinking, which involves sustained, step-by-step analysis, experiments, and insights. You will turn these pages much more slowly than when reading a novel or a newspaper. It may help to have a pencil and paper ready to check claims and carry out experiments.

F As I wrote, I kept in mind two types of readers: those who enjoyed mathematics until they were turned off by an unpleasant episode, usually around fifth grade, and mathematics aficionados, who will find much that is new throughout the book.

This book also serves readers who simply want to sharpen their analytical skills. Many careers, such as law and medicine, require extended, precise analysis. Each chapter offers practice in following a sustained and closely argued line of thought. That mathematics can develop this skill is shown by these two testimonials:

G A physician wrote, 'The discipline of analytical thought processes [in mathematics] prepared me extremely well for medical school. In medicine one is faced with a problem which must be thoroughly analyzed before a solution can be found. The process is similar to doing mathematics.'

A lawyer made the same point, 'Although I had no background in law – not even one political science course – I did well at one of the best law schools. I attribute much of my success there to having learned, through the study of mathematics, and, in particular, theorems, how to analyze complicated principles. Lawyers who have studied mathematics can master the legal principles in a way that most others cannot.'

I hope you will share my delight in watching as simple, even naïve, questions lead to remarkable solutions and purely theoretical discoveries find unanticipated applications.

Questions 27–34

Reading Passage 3 has seven sections, **A–G**.

Which section contains the following information?

*Write the correct letter, **A–G**, in boxes 27–34 on your answer sheet.*

NB *You may use any letter more than once.*

27   a reference to books that assume a lack of mathematical knowledge

28   the way in which this is not a typical book about mathematics

29   personal examples of being helped by mathematics

30   examples of people who each had abilities that seemed incompatible

31   mention of different focuses of books about mathematics

32   a contrast between reading this book and reading other kinds of publication

33   a claim that the whole of the book is accessible to everybody

34   a reference to different categories of intended readers of this book

Questions 35–40

Complete the sentences below.

*Choose **ONE WORD ONLY** from the passage for each answer.*

Write your answers in boxes 35–40 on your answer sheet.

35 Some areas of both music and mathematics are suitable for someone who is a ....

36 It is sometimes possible to understand advanced mathematics using no more than a limited knowledge of ....

37 The writer intends to show that mathematics requires .... thinking, as well as analytical skills.

38 Some books written by .... have had to leave out the mathematics that is central to their theories.

39 The writer advises non-mathematical readers to perform .... while reading the book.

40 A lawyer found that studying .... helped even more than other areas of mathematics in the study of law.

WRITING

WRITING TASK 1

You should spend about 20 minutes on this task.

> *The graph below shows average carbon dioxide (CO$_2$) emissions per person in the United Kingdom, Sweden, Italy and Portugal between 1967 and 2007.*
>
> *Summarise the information by selecting and reporting the main features, and make comparisons where relevant.*

Write at least 150 words.

Average carbon dioxide (CO$_2$) emissions per person, 1967–2007

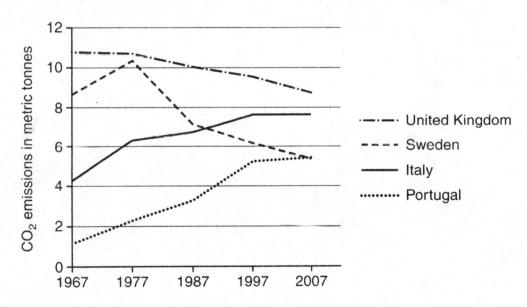

WRITING TASK 2

You should spend about 40 minutes on this task.

Write about the following topic:

> *Some people say that the only reason for learning a foreign language is in order to travel to or work in a foreign country. Others say that these are not the only reasons why someone should learn a foreign language.*
>
> *Discuss both these views and give your own opinion.*

Give reasons for your answer and include any relevant examples from your own knowledge or experience.

Write at least 250 words.

SPEAKING

PART 1

The examiner asks the candidate about him/herself, his/her home, work or studies and other familiar topics.

EXAMPLE

Photographs

- What type of photos do you like taking? [Why/Why not?]
- What do you do with photos you take? [Why/Why not?]
- When you visit other places, do you take photos or buy postcards? [Why/Why not?]
- Do you like people taking photos of you? [Why/Why not?]

PART 2

Describe a day when you thought the weather was perfect.

You should say:
> **where you were on this day**
> **what the weather was like on this day**
> **what you did during the day**
and explain why you thought the weather was perfect on this day.

You will have to talk about the topic for one to two minutes. You have one minute to think about what you are going to say. You can make some notes to help you if you wish.

PART 3

Discussion topics:

Types of weather

Example questions:
What types of weather do people in your country dislike most? Why is that?
What jobs can be affected by different weather conditions? Why?
Are there any important festivals in your country that celebrate a season or type of weather?

Weather forecasts

Example questions:
How important do you think it is for everyone to check what the next day's weather will be? Why?
What is the best way to get accurate information about the weather?
How easy or difficult is it to predict the weather in your country? Why is that?

Test 4

SECTION 1   *Questions 1–10*

Questions 1–7

Complete the table below.

*Write **ONE WORD AND/OR A NUMBER** for each answer*

Event	Cost	Venue	Notes
Jazz band	*Example* Tickets available for £ ......15......	The **1** .... school	Also appearing: Carolyn Hart (plays the **2** ....)
Duck races	£1 per duck	Start behind the **3**	Prize: tickets for **4** .... held at the end of the festival. Ducks can be bought in the **5** ....
Flower show	Free	**6** .... Hall	Prizes presented at 5 pm by a well-known **7** ....

Questions 8–10

Who is each play suitable for?

*Write the correct letter, **A**, **B** or **C**, next to Questions 8–10.*

A	mainly for children
B	mainly for adults
C	suitable for people of all ages

Plays

8   The Mystery of Muldoon   ....

9   Fire and Flood   ....

10   Silly Sailor   ....

SECTION 2   *Questions 11–20*

Questions 11–16

What does the speaker say about each of the following collections?

*Choose **SIX** answers from the box and write the correct letter, **A–G**, next to Questions 11–16.*

Comments
A   was given by one person
B   was recently publicised in the media
C   includes some items given by members of the public
D   includes some items given by the artists
E   includes the most popular exhibits in the museum
F   is the largest of its kind in the country
G   has had some of its contents relocated

Collections

11   20th- and 21st-century paintings   ....

12   19th-century paintings   ....

13   Sculptures   ....

14   'Around the world' exhibition   ....

15   Coins   ....

16   Porcelain and glass   ....

Questions 17–20

Label the plan below.

*Write the correct letter, **A–H**, next to Questions 17–20.*

Basement of museum

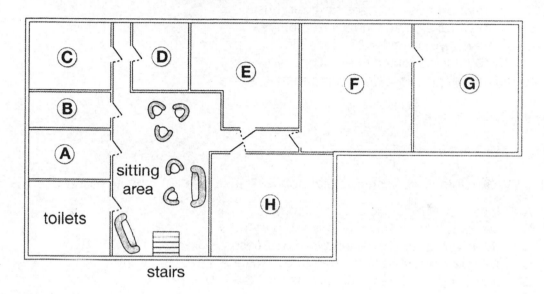

17 restaurant ....

18 café ....

19 baby-changing facilities ....

20 cloakroom ....

SECTION 3   *Questions 21–30*

Questions 21 and 22

*Choose **TWO** letters, **A–E**.*

Which **TWO** characteristics were shared by the subjects of Joanna's psychology study?

    A   They had all won prizes for their music.
    B   They had all made music recordings.
    C   They were all under 27 years old.
    D   They had all toured internationally.
    E   They all played a string instrument.

Questions 23 and 24

*Choose **TWO** letters, **A–E**.*

Which **TWO** points does Joanna make about her use of telephone interviews?

    A   It meant rich data could be collected.
    B   It allowed the involvement of top performers.
    C   It led to a stressful atmosphere at times.
    D   It meant interview times had to be limited.
    E   It caused some technical problems.

Questions 25 and 26

*Choose **TWO** letters, **A–E**.*

Which **TWO** topics did Joanna originally intend to investigate in her research?

    A   regulations concerning concert dress
    B   audience reactions to the dress of performers
    C   changes in performer attitudes to concert dress
    D   how choice of dress relates to performer roles
    E   links between musical instrument and dress choice

Questions 27–30

*Choose the correct letter, **A**, **B** or **C**.*

27   Joanna concentrated on women performers because

    A   women are more influenced by fashion.
    B   women's dress has led to more controversy.
    C   women's code of dress is less strict than men's.

28   Mike Frost's article suggests that in popular music, women's dress is affected by

    A   their wish to be taken seriously.
    B   their tendency to copy each other.
    C   their reaction to the masculine nature of the music.

29   What did Joanna's subjects say about the audience at a performance?

    A   The musicians' choice of clothing is linked to respect for the audience.
    B   The clothing should not distract the audience from the music.
    C   The audience should make the effort to dress appropriately.

30   According to the speakers, musicians could learn from sports scientists about
    A   the importance of clothing for physical freedom.
    B   the part played by clothing in improving performance.
    C   the way clothing may protect against physical injury.

SECTION 4   *Questions 31–40*

Complete the notes below.

*Write **ONE WORD ONLY** for each answer.*

The use of soil to reduce carbon dioxide (CO_2) in the atmosphere

Rattan Lal:
- Claims that 13% of CO_2 in the atmosphere could be absorbed by agricultural soils
- Erosion is more likely in soil that is **31** ....
- Lal found soil in Africa that was very **32** ....
- It was suggested that carbon from soil was entering the atmosphere

Soil and carbon:
- plants turn CO_2 from the air into carbon-based substances such as **33** ....
- some CO_2 moves from the **34** .... of plants to microbes in the soil
- carbon was lost from the soil when agriculture was invented

Regenerative agriculture:
- uses established practices to make sure soil remains fertile and **35** ....
- e.g. through year-round planting and increasing the **36** .... of plants that are grown

California study:
- taking place on a big **37** .... farm
- uses compost made from waste from agriculture and **38** ....

Australia study:
- aims to increase soil carbon by using **39** .... that are always green

Future developments may include:
- reducing the amount of fertilizer used in farming
- giving farmers **40** .... for carbon storage, as well as their produce

READING PASSAGE 1

*You should spend about 20 minutes on **Questions 1–13**, which are based on Reading Passage 1 below.*

Research using twins

To biomedical researchers all over the world, twins offer a precious opportunity to untangle the influence of genes and the environment – of nature and nurture. Because identical twins come from a single fertilized egg that splits into two, they share virtually the same genetic code. Any differences between them – one twin having younger looking skin, for example – must be due to environmental factors such as less time spent in the sun.

Alternatively, by comparing the experiences of identical twins with those of fraternal twins, who come from separate eggs and share on average half their DNA, researchers can quantify the extent to which our genes affect our lives. If identical twins are more similar to each other with respect to an ailment than fraternal twins are, then vulnerability to the disease must be rooted at least in part in heredity.

These two lines of research – studying the differences between identical twins to pinpoint the influence of environment, and comparing identical twins with fraternal ones to measure the role of inheritance – have been crucial to understanding the interplay of nature and nurture in determining our personalities, behavior, and vulnerability to disease.

The idea of using twins to measure the influence of heredity dates back to 1875, when the English scientist Francis Galton first suggested the approach (and coined the phrase 'nature and nurture'). But twin studies took a surprising twist in the 1980s, with the arrival of studies into identical twins who had been separated at birth and reunited as adults. Over two decades 137 sets of twins eventually visited Thomas Bouchard's lab in what became known as the Minnesota Study of Twins Reared Apart. Numerous tests were carried out on the twins, and they were each asked more than 15,000 questions.

Bouchard and his colleagues used this mountain of data to identify how far twins were affected by their genetic makeup. The key to their approach was a statistical concept called heritability. In broad terms, the heritability of a trait measures the extent to which differences among members of a population can be explained by differences in their genetics. And wherever Bouchard and other scientists looked, it seemed, they found the invisible hand of genetic influence helping to shape our lives.

Lately, however, twin studies have helped lead scientists to a radical new conclusion: that nature and nurture are not the only elemental forces at work. According to a recent field called epigenetics, there is a third factor also in play, one that in some cases serves as a bridge between the environment and our genes, and in others operates on its own to shape who we are.

Epigenetic processes are chemical reactions tied to neither nature nor nurture but representing what researchers have called a 'third component'. These reactions influence how our genetic code is expressed: how each gene is strengthened or weakened, even turned on or off, to build our bones, brains and all the other parts of our bodies.

If you think of our DNA as an immense piano keyboard and our genes as the keys – each key symbolizing a segment of DNA responsible for a particular note, or trait, and all the keys combining to make us who we are – then epigenetic processes determine when and how each key can be struck, changing the tune being played.

One way the study of epigenetics is revolutionizing our understanding of biology is by revealing a mechanism by which the environment directly impacts on genes. Studies of animals, for example, have shown that when a rat experiences stress during pregnancy, it can cause epigenetic changes in a fetus that lead to behavioral problems as the rodent grows up. Other epigenetic processes appear to occur randomly, while others are normal, such as those that guide embryonic cells as they become heart, brain, or liver cells, for example.

Geneticist Danielle Reed has worked with many twins over the years and thought deeply about what twin studies have taught us. 'It's very clear when you look at twins that much of what they share is hardwired,' she says. 'Many things about them are absolutely the same and unalterable. But it's also clear, when you get to know them, that other things about them are different. Epigenetics is the origin of a lot of those differences, in my view.'

Reed credits Thomas Bouchard's work for today's surge in twin studies. 'He was the trailblazer,' she says. 'We forget that 50 years ago things like heart disease were thought to be caused entirely by lifestyle. Schizophrenia was thought to be due to poor mothering. Twin studies have allowed us to be more reflective about what people are actually born with and what's caused by experience.'

Having said that, Reed adds, the latest work in epigenetics promises to take our understanding even further. 'What I like to say is that nature writes some things in pencil and some things in pen,' she says. 'Things written in pen you can't change. That's DNA. But things written in pencil you can. That's epigenetics. Now that we're actually able to look at the DNA and see where the pencil writings are, it's sort of a whole new world.'

Questions 1–4

Do the following statements agree with the information given in Reading Passage 1?

In boxes 1–4 on your answer sheet, write

TRUE	*if the statement agrees with the information*
FALSE	*if the statement contradicts the information*
NOT GIVEN	*if there is no information on this*

1   There may be genetic causes for the differences in how young the skin of identical twins looks.

2   Twins are at greater risk of developing certain illnesses than non-twins.

3   Bouchard advertised in newspapers for twins who had been separated at birth.

4   Epigenetic processes are different from both genetic and environmental processes.

Questions 5–9

Look at the following statements (Questions 5–9) and the list of researchers below.

*Match each statement with the correct researcher, **A**, **B** or **C**.*

*Write the correct letter, **A**, **B** or **C**, in boxes 5–9 on your answer sheet.*

NB *You may use any letter more than once.*

List of Researchers
A   Francis Galton
B   Thomas Bouchard
C   Danielle Reed

5   invented a term used to distinguish two factors affecting human characteristics

6   expressed the view that the study of epigenetics will increase our knowledge

7   developed a mathematical method of measuring genetic influences

8   pioneered research into genetics using twins

9   carried out research into twins who had lived apart

Questions 10–13

*Complete the summary using the list of words, **A–F**, below.*

*Write the correct letter, **A–F**, in boxes 10–13 on your answer sheet.*

Epigenetic processes

In epigenetic processes, **10** .... influence the activity of our genes, for example in creating our internal **11** .... The study of epigenetic processes is uncovering a way in which our genes can be affected by our **12** .... One example is that if a pregnant rat suffers stress, the new-born rat may later show problems in its **13** ....

A nurture	**B** organs	**C** code
D chemicals	**E** environment	**F** behaviour/behavior

READING PASSAGE 2

*You should spend about 20 minutes on **Questions 14–26**, which are based on Reading Passage 2 below.*

An Introduction to Film Sound

Though we might think of film as an essentially visual experience, we really cannot afford to underestimate the importance of film sound. A meaningful sound track is often as complicated as the image on the screen, and is ultimately just as much the responsibility of the director. The entire sound track consists of three essential ingredients: the human voice, sound effects and music. These three tracks must be mixed and balanced so as to produce the necessary emphases which in turn create desired effects. Topics which essentially refer to the three previously mentioned tracks are discussed below. They include dialogue, synchronous and asynchronous sound effects, and music.

Let us start with dialogue. As is the case with stage drama, dialogue serves to tell the story and expresses feelings and motivations of characters as well. Often with film characterization the audience perceives little or no difference between the character and the actor. Thus, for example, the actor Humphrey Bogart is the character Sam Spade; film personality and life personality seem to merge. Perhaps this is because the very texture of a performer's voice supplies an element of character.

When voice textures fit the performer's physiognomy and gestures, a whole and very realistic persona emerges. The viewer sees not an actor working at his craft, but another human being struggling with life. It is interesting to note that how dialogue is used and the very amount of dialogue used varies widely among films. For example, in the highly successful science-fiction film *2001*, little dialogue was evident, and most of it was banal and of little intrinsic interest. In this way the film-maker was able to portray what Thomas Sobochack and Vivian Sobochack call, in *An Introduction to Film*, the 'inadequacy of human responses when compared with the magnificent technology created by man and the visual beauties of the universe'.

The comedy *Bringing Up Baby*, on the other hand, presents practically non-stop dialogue delivered at breakneck speed. This use of dialogue underscores not only the dizzy quality of the character played by Katherine Hepburn, but also the absurdity of the film itself and thus its humor. The audience is bounced from gag to gag and conversation to conversation; there is no time for audience reflection. The audience is caught up in a whirlwind of activity in simply managing to follow the plot. This film presents pure escapism – largely due to its frenetic dialogue.

Synchronous sound effects are those sounds which are synchronized or matched with what is viewed. For example, if the film portrays a character playing the piano, the sounds of the piano are projected. Synchronous sounds contribute to the realism of film and also help to create a particular atmosphere. For example, the 'click' of a door being opened may simply serve to convince the audience that the image portrayed is real, and the audience may only subconsciously note the expected sound. However, if the 'click' of an opening door is part of an ominous action such as a burglary, the sound mixer may call attention to the 'click' with an increase in volume; this helps to engage the audience in a moment of suspense.

Asynchronous sound effects, on the other hand, are not matched with a visible source of the sound on screen. Such sounds are included so as to provide an appropriate emotional nuance, and they may also add to the realism of the film. For example, a film-maker might opt to include the background sound of an ambulance's siren while the foreground sound and image portrays an arguing couple. The asynchronous ambulance siren underscores the psychic injury incurred in the argument; at the same time the noise of the siren adds to the realism of the film by acknowledging the film's city setting.

We are probably all familiar with background music in films, which has become so ubiquitous as to be noticeable in its absence. We are aware that it is used to add emotion and rhythm. Usually not meant to be noticeable, it often provides a tone or an emotional attitude toward the story and/or the characters depicted. In addition, background music often foreshadows a change in mood. For example, dissonant music may be used in film to indicate an approaching (but not yet visible) menace or disaster.

Background music may aid viewer understanding by linking scenes. For example, a particular musical theme associated with an individual character or situation may be repeated at various points in a film in order to remind the audience of salient motifs or ideas.

Film sound comprises conventions and innovations. We have come to expect an acceleration of music during car chases and creaky doors in horror films. Yet, it is important to note as well that sound is often brilliantly conceived. The effects of sound are often largely subtle and often are noted by only our subconscious minds. We need to foster an awareness of film sound as well as film space so as to truly appreciate an art form that sprang to life during the twentieth century – the modern film.

Questions 14–18

*Choose the correct letter, **A**, **B**, **C** or **D**.*

Write the correct letter in boxes 14–18 on your answer sheet.

14   In the first paragraph, the writer makes a point that

   A   the director should plan the sound track at an early stage in filming.
   B   it would be wrong to overlook the contribution of sound to the artistry of films.
   C   the music industry can have a beneficial influence on sound in film.
   D   it is important for those working on the sound in a film to have sole responsibility for it.

15   One reason that the writer refers to Humphrey Bogart is to exemplify

   A   the importance of the actor and the character appearing to have similar personalities.
   B   the audience's wish that actors are visually appropriate for their roles.
   C   the value of the actor having had similar feelings to the character.
   D   the audience's preference for dialogue to be as authentic as possible.

16   In the third paragraph, the writer suggests that

   A   audiences are likely to be critical of film dialogue that does not reflect their own experience.
   B   film dialogue that appears to be dull may have a specific purpose.
   C   filmmakers vary considerably in the skill with which they handle dialogue.
   D   the most successful films are those with dialogue of a high quality.

17   What does the writer suggest about *Bringing Up Baby*?

   A   The plot suffers from the filmmaker's wish to focus on humorous dialogue.
   B   The dialogue helps to make it one of the best comedy films ever produced.
   C   There is a mismatch between the speed of the dialogue and the speed of actions.
   D   The nature of the dialogue emphasises key elements of the film.

18   The writer refers to the 'click' of a door to make the point that realistic sounds

   A   are often used to give the audience a false impression of events in the film.
   B   may be interpreted in different ways by different members of the audience.
   C   may be modified in order to manipulate the audience's response to the film.
   D   tend to be more significant in films presenting realistic situations.

Questions 19–23

Do the following statements agree with the information given in Reading Passage 2?

In boxes 19–23 on your answer sheet, write

> **TRUE**   *if the statement agrees with the information*
> **FALSE**   *if the statement contradicts the information*
> **NOT GIVEN**   *if there is no information on this*

19   Audiences are likely to be surprised if a film lacks background music.

20   Background music may anticipate a development in a film.

21   Background music has more effect on some people than on others.

22   Background music may help the audience to make certain connections within the film.

23   Audiences tend to be aware of how the background music is affecting them.

Questions 24–26

*Complete each sentence with the correct ending, **A–E**, below.*

*Write the correct letter, **A–E**, in boxes 24–26 on your answer sheet.*

24   The audience's response to different parts of a film can be controlled

25   The feelings and motivations of characters become clear

26   A character seems to be a real person rather than an actor

---

A   when the audience listens to the dialogue.

B   if the film reflects the audience's own concerns.

C   if voice, sound and music are combined appropriately.

D   when the director is aware of how the audience will respond.

E   when the actor's appearance, voice and moves are consistent with each other.

READING PASSAGE 3

*You should spend about 20 minutes on **Questions 27–40**, which are based on Reading Passage 3 on the following pages.*

Questions 27–32

Reading Passage 3 has six paragraphs, **A–F**.

*Choose the correct heading for paragraphs **A–F** from the list of headings below.*

*Write the correct number, **i–vii**, in boxes 27–32 on your answer sheet.*

	List of Headings
i	Differences between languages highlight their impressiveness
ii	The way in which a few sounds are organised to convey a huge range of meaning
iii	Why the sounds used in different languages are not identical
iv	Apparently incompatible characteristics of language
v	Even silence can be meaningful
vi	Why language is the most important invention of all
vii	The universal ability to use language

27   Paragraph **A**

28   Paragraph **B**

29   Paragraph **C**

30   Paragraph **D**

31   Paragraph **E**

32   Paragraph **F**

'This Marvellous Invention'

A Of all mankind's manifold creations, language must take pride of place. Other inventions – the wheel, agriculture, sliced bread – may have transformed our material existence, but the advent of language is what made us human. Compared to language, all other inventions pale in significance, since everything we have ever achieved depends on language and originates from it. Without language, we could never have embarked on our ascent to unparalleled power over all other animals, and even over nature itself.

B But language is foremost not just because it came first. In its own right it is a tool of extraordinary sophistication, yet based on an idea of ingenious simplicity: 'this marvellous invention of composing out of twenty-five or thirty sounds that infinite variety of expressions which, whilst having in themselves no likeness to what is in our mind, allow us to disclose to others its whole secret, and to make known to those who cannot penetrate it all that we imagine, and all the various stirrings of our soul'. This was how, in 1660, the renowned French grammarians of the Port-Royal abbey near Versailles distilled the essence of language, and no one since has celebrated more eloquently the magnitude of its achievement. Even so, there is just one flaw in all these hymns of praise, for the homage to language's unique accomplishment conceals a simple yet critical incongruity. Language is mankind's greatest invention – except, of course, that it was never invented. This apparent paradox is at the core of our fascination with language, and it holds many of its secrets.

C Language often seems so skillfully drafted that one can hardly imagine it as anything other than the perfected handiwork of a master craftsman. How else could this instrument make so much out of barely three dozen measly morsels of sound? In themselves, these configurations of mouth – *p,f,b,v,t,d,k,g,sh,a,e* and so on – amount to nothing more than a few haphazard spits and splutters, random noises with no meaning, no ability to express, no power to explain. But run them through the cogs and wheels of the language machine, let it arrange them in some very special orders, and there is nothing that these meaningless streams of air cannot do: from sighing the interminable boredom of existence to unravelling the fundamental order of the universe.

D The most extraordinary thing about language, however, is that one doesn't have to be a genius to set its wheels in motion. The language machine allows just about everybody – from pre-modern foragers in the subtropical savannah, to post-modern philosophers in the suburban sprawl – to tie these meaningless sounds together into an infinite variety of subtle senses, and all apparently without the slightest exertion. Yet it is precisely this deceptive ease which makes language a victim of its own success, since in everyday life its triumphs are usually taken for granted. The wheels of language run so smoothly that one rarely bothers to stop and think about all the resourcefulness and expertise that must have gone into making it tick. Language conceals art.

E   Often, it is only the estrangement of foreign tongues, with their many exotic and outlandish features, that brings home the wonder of language's design. One of the showiest stunts that some languages can pull off is an ability to build up words of breath-breaking length, and thus express in one word what English takes a whole sentence to say. The Turkish word *şehirlileştiremediklerimizdensiniz*, to take one example, means nothing less than 'you are one of those whom we can't turn into a town-dweller'. (In case you were wondering, this monstrosity really is one word, not merely many different words squashed together – most of its components cannot even stand up on their own.)

F   And if that sounds like some one-off freak, then consider Sumerian, the language spoken on the banks of the Euphrates some 5,000 years ago by the people who invented writing and thus enabled the documentation of history. A Sumerian word like *munintuma'a* ('when he had made it suitable for her') might seem rather trim compared to the Turkish colossus above. What is so impressive about it, however, is not its lengthiness but rather the reverse – the thrifty compactness of its construction. The word is made up of different slots, each corresponding to a particular portion of meaning. This sleek design allows single sounds to convey useful information, and in fact even the absence of a sound has been enlisted to express something specific. If you were to ask which bit in the Sumerian word corresponds to the pronoun 'it' in the English translation 'when he had made it suitable for her', then the answer would have to be nothing. Mind you, a very particular kind of nothing: the nothing that stands in the empty slot in the middle. The technology is so fine-tuned then that even a non-sound, when carefully placed in a particular position, has been invested with a specific function. Who could possibly have come up with such a nifty contraption?

Questions 33–36

*Complete the summary using the list of words, **A–G**, below.*

*Write the correct letter, **A–G**, in boxes 33–36 on your answer sheet.*

The importance of language

The wheel is one invention that has had a major impact on **33** .... aspects of life, but no impact has been as **34** .... as that of language. Language is very **35** .... , yet composed of just a small number of sounds.

Language appears to be **36** .... to use. However, its sophistication is often overlooked.

A	difficult	**B**	complex	**C**	original
D	admired	**E**	material	**F**	easy
G	fundamental				

Questions 37–40

Do the following statements agree with the views of the writer in Reading Passage 3?

In boxes 37–40 on your answer sheet, write

YES	*if the statement agrees with the views of the writer*
NO	*if the statement contradicts the views of the writer*
NOT GIVEN	*if it is impossible to say what the writer thinks about this*

37   Human beings might have achieved their present position without language.

38   The Port-Royal grammarians did justice to the nature of language.

39   A complex idea can be explained more clearly in a sentence than in a single word.

40   The Sumerians were responsible for starting the recording of events.

WRITING

WRITING TASK 1

You should spend about 20 minutes on this task.

> *The table below shows the numbers of visitors to Ashdown Museum during the year before and the year after it was refurbished. The charts show the result of surveys asking visitors how satisfied they were with their visit, during the same two periods.*
>
> *Summarise the information by selecting and reporting the main features, and make comparisons where relevant.*

Write at least 150 words.

Total number of visitors to Ashdown Museum	
During the year before refurbishment:	74,000
During the year after refurbishment:	92,000

Results of surveys of visitor satisfaction

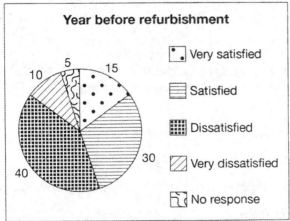

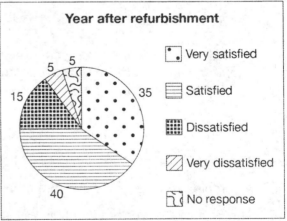

WRITING TASK 2

You should spend about 40 minutes on this task.

Write about the following topic:

> *Many governments think that economic progress is their most important goal. Some people, however, think that other types of progress are equally important for a country.*
>
> *Discuss both these views and give your own opinion.*

Give reasons for your answer and include any relevant examples from your own knowledge or experience.

Write at least 250 words.

SPEAKING

PART 1

The examiner asks the candidate about him/herself, his/her home, work or studies and other familiar topics.

EXAMPLE

Names

- How did your parents choose your name(s)?
- Does your name have any special meaning?
- Is your name common or unusual in your country?
- If you could change your name, would you? [Why/Why not?]

PART 2

Describe a TV documentary you watched that was particularly interesting.

You should say:
> **what the documentary was about**
> **why you decided to watch it**
> **what you learnt during the documentary**
and explain why the TV documentary was particularly interesting.

You will have to talk about the topic for one to two minutes. You have one minute to think about what you are going to say. You can make some notes to help you if you wish.

PART 3

Discussion topics:

Different types of TV programmes

Example questions:
What are the most popular kinds of TV programmes in your country? Why is this?
Do you think there are too many game shows on TV nowadays? Why?
Do you think TV is the main way for people to get the news in your country? What other ways are there?

TV advertising

Example questions:
What types of products are advertised most often on TV?
Do you think that people pay attention to adverts on TV? Why do you think that is?
How important are regulations on TV advertising?

Audioscripts

SECTION 1

OFFICIAL:	Hello?
WOMAN:	Oh, hello. I wanted to enquire about hiring a room in the Village Hall, for the evening of September the first.
OFFICIAL:	Let me just see … Yes, we have both rooms available that evening. There's our Main Hall – that's got seating for <u>200</u> people. Or there's the Charlton Room …
WOMAN:	Sorry?
OFFICIAL:	The <u>Charlton</u> Room – C-H-A-R L-T-O-N. That's got seating for up to one hundred.
WOMAN:	Well, we're organising a dinner to raise money for a charity, and we're hoping for at least 150 people, so I think we'll go for the Main Hall. How much would that cost?
OFFICIAL:	Let's see. You wanted it for the evening of September 1st?
WOMAN:	Yes, that's a Saturday.
OFFICIAL:	So from six pm to midnight that'd be £<u>115</u> – that's the weekend price, it's £75 on weekdays.
WOMAN:	That's all right.
OFFICIAL:	And I have to tell you there's also a deposit of £250, which is returnable of course as long as there's no damage. But we do insist that this is <u>paid in cash</u>, we don't take cards for that. You can pay the actual rent of the room however you like though – cash, credit card, cheque …
WOMAN:	Oh, well I suppose that's OK. So does the charge include use of tables and chairs and so on?
OFFICIAL:	Oh, yes.
WOMAN:	<u>And what about parking?</u>
OFFICIAL:	<u>Yeah, that's all included</u>. The only thing that isn't included is … you said you were organising a dinner?
WOMAN:	Yeah.
OFFICIAL:	Well, you'll have to pay extra for the kitchen if you want to use that. It's £25. It's got very good facilities – good quality cookers and fridges and so on.
WOMAN:	OK, well I suppose that's all right. We can cover the cost in our entry charges.
OFFICIAL:	Right. So I'll make a note of that. Now there are just one or two things you need to think about before the event. For example, <u>you'll have to see about getting a licence if you're planning to have any music during the meal</u>.
WOMAN:	Oh, really?
OFFICIAL:	It's quite straightforward, I'll give you the details later on. And about a week or ten days before your event you'll need to contact the caretaker, that's Mr Evans, <u>to make the arrangements for entry</u> – he'll sort that out with you.
WOMAN:	And do I give him the payment as well?
OFFICIAL:	No, you do that directly with me.

WOMAN:	Right. Now is there anything I need to know about what happens during the event?
OFFICIAL:	Well, as you'll be aware, of course the building is no smoking throughout.
WOMAN:	Of course.

Example

Q1

Q2

Q3

Q4

Q5

Q6

OFFICIAL: Now, are you having a band?
WOMAN: Yes.
OFFICIAL: Well, they'll have a lot of equipment, so rather than using the front door they should park their van round the back and use the stage door there. You can open that from inside but don't forget to lock it at the end. *Q7*
WOMAN: OK.
OFFICIAL: And talking of bands, I'm sure I don't need to tell you this, but you must make sure that no one fiddles about with the black box by the fire door – that's a system that cuts in when the volume reaches a certain level. It's a legal requirement.
WOMAN: Sure. Anyway, we want people to be able to talk to one another so we don't want anything too loud. Oh, that reminds me, we'll be having speeches – are there any microphones available?
OFFICIAL: Yeah. Just let the caretaker know, he'll get those for you. Right, now when the event is over we do ask that the premises are left in good condition. So there's a locked cupboard and you'll be informed of the code you need to open that. It's got all the cleaning equipment, brushes and detergent and so on. *Q8*
WOMAN: Right. So what do we need to do after everyone's gone? Sweep the floors I suppose?
OFFICIAL: Well, actually they have to be washed, not just swept. Then you'll be provided with black plastic bags, so all the rubbish must be collected up and left outside the door. *Q9*
WOMAN: Of course. We'll make sure everything's left tidy. Oh, and I forgot to ask, I presume we can have decorations in the room?
OFFICIAL: Yes, but you must take them down afterwards. *Q10*
WOMAN: Sure.
OFFICIAL: And the chairs and tables should be stacked up neatly at the back of the room
WOMAN: I'll make sure I've got a few people to help me.

SECTION 2

Welcome to the Fiddy Working Heritage Farm. This open-air museum gives you the experience of agriculture and rural life in the English countryside at the end of the nineteenth century. So you'll see a typical farm of that period, and like me, all the staff are dressed in clothes of that time.

I must give you some advice and safety tips before we go any further. As it's a *working farm*, please don't frighten or injure the animals. We have a lot here, and many of them are breeds that are now quite rare. *Q11*

And do stay at a safe distance from the tools: some of them have sharp points which can be pretty dangerous, so please don't touch them. We don't want any accidents, do we? *Q12*

The ground is very uneven, and you might slip if you're wearing sandals so I'm glad to see you're all wearing shoes – we always advise people to do that. *Q13*

Now, children of all ages are very welcome here, and usually even very young children love the ducks and lambs, so do bring them along next time you come.

I don't think any of you have brought dogs with you, but in case you have, I'm afraid they'll have to stay in the car park, unless they're guide dogs. I'm sure you'll understand that they could cause a lot of problems on a farm. *Q14*

Now let me give you some idea of the layout of the farm. The building where you bought your tickets is the New Barn, immediately to your right, and we're now at the beginning of the main path to the farmland – and of course the car park is on your left. <u>The scarecrow you can see in the car park in the corner, beside the main path</u>, is a traditional figure for keeping the birds away from crops, but our scarecrow is a permanent sculpture. It's taller than a human being, so you can see it from quite a distance. *Q15*

<u>If you look ahead of you, you'll see a maze. It's opposite the New Barn, beside the side path that branches off to the right just over there</u>. The maze is made out of hedges which are too tall for young children to see over them, but it's quite small, so you can't get lost in it! *Q16*

Now, can you see the bridge crossing the fish pool further up the main path? <u>If you want to go to the café, go towards the bridge and turn right just before it. Walk along the side path and the café's on the first bend you come to</u>. The building was originally the schoolhouse, and it's well over a hundred years old. *Q17*

As you may know, we run skills workshops here, where you can learn traditional crafts like woodwork and basket-making. You can see examples of the work, and talk to someone about the courses, in the Black Barn. <u>If you take the side path to the right, here, just by the New Barn, you'll come to the Black Barn just where the path first bends</u>. *Q18*

Now I mustn't forget to tell you about picnicking, as I can see some of you have brought your lunch with you. You can picnic in the field, though do clear up behind you, of course. <u>Or if you'd prefer a covered picnic area, there's one near the farmyard: just after you cross the bridge, there's a covered picnic spot on the right</u>. *Q19*

And the last thing to mention is <u>Fiddy House itself. From here you can cross the bridge then walk along the footpath through the field to the left of the farmyard. That goes to the house</u>, and it'll give you a lovely view of it. It's certainly worth a few photographs, but as it's a private home, I'm afraid you can't go inside. *Q20*

Right. Well, if you're all ready, we'll set off on our tour of the farm.

SECTION 3

LISA: OK, Greg, so I finally managed to read the article you mentioned – the one about the study on gender in physics.

GREG: About the study of college students done by Akira Miyake and his team? Yeah. I was interested that the researchers were actually a mix of psychologists and physicists. That's an unusual combination.

LISA: Yeah. I got a little confused at first about which students the study was based on. They weren't actually majoring in physics – <u>they were majoring in what's known as the STEM disciplines. That's science, technology, engineering and …</u> *Q21*

GREG: … and math. Yes, but they were all doing physics courses as part of their studies.

LISA: That's correct. So as I understood it, Miyake and co started from the fact that women are underrepresented in introductory physics courses at college, and also that on average, the women who do enrol on these courses perform more poorly than the men. No one really knows why this is the case.

GREG: Yeah. <u>But what the researchers wanted to find out was basically what they could do about the relatively low level of the women's results.</u> But in order to find a solution they needed to find out more about the nature of the problem. *Q22*

LISA: Right – now let's see if I can remember … it was that in the physics class, the female students thought the male students all assumed that women weren't any good at physics … was that it? And they thought that the men expected them to get poor results in their tests.

105

GREG: That's what the women thought, and that made them nervous, so they did get poor results. <u>But actually they were wrong … No one was making any assumptions about the female students at all</u>.　　*Q23*

LISA: Anyway, what Miyake's team did was quite simple – getting the students to do some writing before they went into the physics class. What did they call it?

GREG: Values-affirmation – <u>they had to write an essay focusing on things that were significant to them, not particularly to do with the subject they were studying, but more general things like music, or people who mattered to them</u>.　　*Q24*

LISA: Right. So the idea of doing the writing is that this gets the students thinking in a positive way.

GREG: <u>And putting these thoughts into words can relax them and help them overcome the psychological factors that lead to poor performance</u>. Yeah. <u>But what the researchers in the study hadn't expected was that this one activity raised the women's physics grades from the C to the B range</u>.　　*Q25*　*Q26*

LISA: A huge change. Pity it wasn't to an A, but still! No, but it does suggest that the women were seriously underperforming beforehand, in comparison with the men.

GREG: Yes. Mind you, Miyake's article left out a lot of details. Like, did the students do the writing just once, or several times? <u>And had they been told why they were doing the writing? That might have affected the results</u>.　　*Q27*

LISA: You mean, if they know the researchers thought it might help them to improve, then they'd just try to fulfil that expectation?

GREG: Exactly.

GREG: So anyway, I thought for our project we could do a similar study, but investigate whether it really was the writing activity that had that result.

LISA: OK. So we could ask them to do a writing task about something completely different … something more factual? Like a general knowledge topic.

GREG: Maybe … or we could have half the students doing a writing task and half doing something else, like an oral task.

LISA: Or even, <u>half do the same writing task as in the original research and half do a factual writing task</u>. Then we'd see if it really is the topic that made the difference, or something else.　　*Q28*

GREG: That's it. Good. So at our meeting with the supervisor on Monday we can tell him we've decided on our project. We should have our aims ready by then. I suppose we need to read the original study – the article's just a summary.

LISA: And there was another article I read, by Smolinsky. It was about her research on how women and men perform in mixed teams in class, compared with single-sex teams and on their own.

GREG: Let me guess … the women were better at teamwork.

LISA: That's what I expected, but actually <u>the men and the women got the same results whether they were working in teams or on their own</u>. But I guess it's not that relevant to us.　　*Q29*

GREG: What worries me anyway is how we're going to get everything done in the time.

LISA: We'll be OK now we know what we're doing. Though I'm not clear how we assess whether the students in our experiment actually make any progress or not …

GREG: No. We may need some advice on that. The main thing's to make sure we have the right size sample, not too big or too small.

LISA: That shouldn't be difficult. Right, what do we need to do next? We could have a look at the timetable for the science classes … or perhaps <u>we should just make an appointment to see one of the science professors. That'd be better</u>.　　*Q30*

GREG: Great. And we could even get to observe one of the classes.

LISA: What for?

GREG: Well … OK maybe let's just go with your idea. Right, well …

SECTION 4

I've been looking at ocean biodiversity, that's the diversity of species that live in the world's oceans. About 20 years ago biologists developed the idea of what they called 'biodiversity hotspots'. These are the areas which have the greatest mixture of species, so one example is Madagascar. These hotspots are significant because they allow us to locate key areas for focusing efforts at conservation. Biologists can identify hotspots on land, fairly easily, but until recently, very little was known about species distribution and diversity in the oceans, and no one even knew if hotspots existed there. *Q31*

Then a Canadian biologist called Boris Worm did some research in 2005 on data on ocean species that he got from the fishing industry. Worm located five hotspots for large ocean predators like sharks, and looked at what they had in common. The main thing he'd expected to find was that they had very high concentrations of food, but to his surprise that was only true for four of the hotspots – the remaining hotspot was quite badly off in that regard. But what he did find was that in all cases, the water at the surface of the ocean had relatively high temperatures, even when it was cool at greater depths, so this seemed to be a factor in supporting a diverse range of these large predators. However, this wasn't enough on its own, because he also found that the water needed to have enough oxygen in it – so these two factors seemed necessary to support the high metabolic rate of these large fish. *Q32* *Q33* *Q34*

A couple of years later, in 2007, a researcher called Lisa Ballance, who was working in California, also started looking for ocean hotspots, but not for fish – what she was interested in was marine mammals, things like seals. And she found three places in the oceans which were hotspots, and what these had in common was that these hotspots were all located at boundaries between ocean currents, and this seems to be the sort of place that has lots of the plankton that some of these species feed on. *Q35*

So now people who want to protect the species that are endangered need to get as much information as possible. For example, there's an international project called the Census of Marine Life. They've been surveying oceans all over the world, including the Arctic. One thing they found there which stunned other researchers was that there were large numbers of species which live below the ice – sometimes under a layer up to 20 metres thick. Some of these species had never been seen before. They've even found species of octopus living in these conditions. And other scientists working on the same project, but researching very different habitats on the ocean floor, have found large numbers of species congregating around volcanoes, attracted to them by the warmth and nutrients there. *Q36*

However, biologists still don't know how serious the threat to their survival is for each individual species. So a body called the Global Marine Species Assessment is now creating a list of endangered species on land, so they consider things like the size of the population – how many members of one species there are in a particular place – and then they look at their distribution in geographical terms, although this is quite difficult when you're looking at fish, because they're so mobile, and then thirdly they calculate the rate at which the decline of the species is happening. *Q37*

So far only 1,500 species have been assessed, but they want to increase this figure to 20,000. For each one they assess, they use the data they collect on that species to produce a map showing its distribution. Ultimately they will be able to use these to figure out not only where most species are located but also where they are most threatened. *Q38*

So finally, what can be done to retain the diversity of species in the world's oceans? Firstly, we need to set up more reserves in our oceans, places where marine species are protected. We have some, but not enough. In addition, to preserve species such as leatherback turtles,

which live out in the high seas but have their nesting sites on the American coast, <u>we need</u>   *Q39*
<u>to create corridors for migration</u>, so they can get from one area to another safely. As well as this, action needs to be taken to lower the levels of fishing quotas to prevent overfishing of endangered species. And finally, there's the problem of 'by-catch'. This refers to the catching of unwanted fish by fishing boats – they're returned to the sea, but they're often dead or dying. If these commercial fishing boats used equipment which was more selective, <u>so that</u>   *Q40*
<u>only the fish wanted for consumption were caught</u>, this problem could be overcome.

OK. So does anyone have any …

TEST 2

SECTION 1

CAROLINE: Good Morning. Youth Council. Caroline speaking.

ROGER: Oh, hello, I'm interested in standing for election to the Youth Council, and I was told to give you a call.

CAROLINE: That's good. Could I have your name, please?

ROGER: Yes, it's Roger <u>Brown</u>.   *Example*

CAROLINE: Thank you. I'm Caroline, the Youth Council administrator. So do you know much about what the Council does, Roger?

ROGER: I've talked to Stephanie – I think she's the chair of the Council.

CAROLINE: That's right.

ROGER: And she told me a lot about it. How it's a way for young people to discuss local issues, for example, and make suggestions to the town council. That's what made me interested.

CAROLINE: Fine. Well let me take down some of your details. First of all, how old are you? You know the Council is for young people aged from 13 to 18?

ROGER: I've just turned 18.

CAROLINE: And where do you live, Roger?

ROGER: Well, that's a bit complicated. At the moment I'm looking for a flat to rent here, so <u>I'm in a hostel from Monday to Friday</u>. I go back to my parents' place at the   *Q1*
weekend.

CAROLINE: OK, so where's the best place to send you some information about the Council?

ROGER: Oh, to my parents' address, please. That's 17, <u>Buckleigh</u> Street – B-U-C-K-L-E-I-   *Q2*
G-H Street, Stamford, Lincolnshire, though you don't really need the county.

CAROLINE: Oh, I know Stamford – it's a lovely town. And what's the postcode?

ROGER: <u>PE9 7QT</u>   *Q3*

CAROLINE: Right, thank you. So are you working here, or are you a student?

ROGER: I started studying at the university a couple of weeks ago, and I've got a part-time job for a few hours a week.

CAROLINE: What do you do?

ROGER: Well, I've done several different things. I've just finished a short-term contract as a courier, and now <u>I'm working as a waiter</u> in one of the big hotels.   *Q4*

CAROLINE: Uhuh. That can't leave you much time for studying!

ROGER: Oh, it's not too bad. I manage to fit it all in.

CAROLINE: What are you studying?

ROGER: My ambition is to go into parliament eventually, so <u>my major subject is politics</u>.   *Q5*
That's partly why I think the Youth Council is important and want to be a part of it.

CAROLINE:	And I suppose you're also taking a minor subject, aren't you? I know a lot of people study economics too.
ROGER:	I chose history. To be honest, I'm not finding it as interesting as I expected!

CAROLINE:	OK, so with your studying and your part-time job, do you have time for any other interests or hobbies?	
ROGER:	Well, <u>I spend quite a lot of time cycling</u> – both around town to get to university and to work, and also long-distance, from here to London, for instance.	Q6
CAROLINE:	That's pretty impressive! Anything else?	
ROGER:	For relaxation <u>I'm also keen on the cinema</u> – I used to go at least once a week, but I can't manage to go so often now.	Q7
CAROLINE:	Right. Are you sure you'll have enough time for the Youth Council?	
ROGER:	Yes, I've worked out that I can afford to reduce my hours at work, and that will make the time.	
CAROLINE:	So is there any particular aspect of the Youth Council's work that appeals to you, Roger?	
ROGER:	Well, my sister is blind, so <u>I'm particularly interested in working with disabled young people</u>, to try and improve the quality of their lives.	Q8
CAROLINE:	That's great. Well, the best way to get involved is to be nominated by some people who you know.	
ROGER:	Right. Can you tell me how to set about organising that?	
CAROLINE:	You should talk to Jeffrey, our Elections Officer. I can arrange a meeting in the council office with him, if you like.	
ROGER:	Yes, please.	
CAROLINE:	He'll be here next Monday, if that suits you.	
ROGER:	That's the 14th, isn't it?	
CAROLINE:	Yes.	
ROGER:	I can manage late afternoon.	
CAROLINE:	Would you like to suggest a time? He generally leaves around 5.30.	
ROGER:	Well, <u>would 4.30 be OK</u>? My last class finishes at 4, so I'd have plenty of time to get to your office.	Q9
CAROLINE:	Right, that's fine. Oh, and could I have a phone number we can contact you on?	
ROGER:	Yes, <u>my mobile number's 07788 136711</u>.	Q10
CAROLINE:	Thank you. Well, we'll look forward to seeing you next week.	
ROGER:	Thanks very much. Goodbye.	
CAROLINE:	Bye.	

SECTION 2

Hi. Great to see you! I'm Jody, and I'll be looking after both of you for the first month you're working here at the Amersham Theatre. I'll tell you something about the theatre now, then take you to meet two of the other staff.

It's an old building, and it's been modernised several times. In fact, as you can see, we're carrying out a major refurbishment at the moment. The interior has just been repainted, and we're about to start on the exterior of the building – that'll be a big job. The work's running over budget, so we've had to postpone installing an elevator. I hope you're happy running up and down stairs! When the theatre was built, people were generally slimmer and shorter than now, and the seats were very close together. <u>We've replaced them with larger seats, with more legroom. This means fewer seats in total, but we've taken the opportunity to install seats that can easily be moved</u>, to create different acting spaces. <u>We've also turned a few</u>   Q11 & 12   Q11 & 12 storerooms over to other purposes, like using them for meetings.

We try hard to involve members of the public in the theatre. <u>One way is by organising backstage tours, so people can be shown round the building and learn how a theatre operates. These are proving very popular.</u> What we're finding is that people want to have lunch or a cup of coffee while they're here, so we're looking into the possibility of opening a café in due course. <u>We have a bookshop, which specialises in books about drama, and that attracts plenty of customers.</u> Then there are two large rooms that will be decorated next month, and they'll be available for hire, for conferences and private functions, such as parties. We're also considering hiring out costumes to amateur drama clubs.

Q13 & 14

Q13 & 14

Now I want to tell you about our workshops. We recently started a programme of workshops that anyone can join. Eventually we intend to run courses in acting, but we're waiting until we've got the right people in place as trainers. That's proving more difficult than we'd expected! There's a big demand to learn about the technical side of putting on a production, and <u>our lighting workshop has already started, with great success</u>. We're going to start one on sound next month. A number of people have enquired about workshops on make-up, and that's something we're considering for the future. <u>A surprise success is the workshop on making puppets – we happen to have someone working here who does it as a hobby, and she offered to run a workshop. It was so popular we're now running them every month!</u>

Q15 & 16

Q15 & 16

Now, a word about the layout of the building. The auditorium, stage and dressing rooms for the actors are all below ground level. Here on the ground floor we have most of the rooms that the public doesn't see. The majority are internal, so they have windows in the roof to light them.

Standing here in the foyer, you're probably wondering why the box office isn't here, where the public would expect to find it. Well, you might have noticed it on your way in – although <u>it's part of this building, it's next door, with a separate entrance from the road.</u>

Q17

<u>For the theatre manager's office, you go across the foyer and through the double doors, turn right, and it's the room at the end of the corridor, with the door on the left.</u>

Q18

<u>The lighting box is where the computerised stage lighting is operated, and it's at the back of the building. When you're through the double doors, turn left, turn right at the water cooler, and right again at the end. It's the second room along that corridor.</u> The lighting box has a window into the auditorium, which of course is below us.

Q19

<u>The artistic director's office is through the double doors, turn right, and it's the first room you come to on the right-hand side.</u> And finally, for the moment, the room where I'll take you next – the relaxation room. So if you'd like to come with me …

Q20

SECTION 3

HELEN: I've brought my notes on our Biology Field Trip to Rocky Bay, Colin, so we can work on our report on the research we did together.

COLIN: OK. I've got mine too. Let's look at the aims of the trip first.

HELEN: Right. What did you have?

COLIN: I just put something about getting experience of the different sorts of procedures used on a field trip. But <u>we need something about what causes different organisms to choose particular habitats.</u>

Q21

HELEN: <u>I agree.</u> And something about finding out how to protect organisms in danger of dying out?

COLIN:	In our aims? But we weren't really looking at that.
HELEN:	I suppose not. OK, now there's the list of equipment we all had to bring on the field trip. What did they tell us to bring a ruler for?
COLIN.	It was something about measuring the slope of the shore, but of course we didn't need it because we were measuring wind direction, and we'd brought the compass for that …
HELEN:	But not the piece of string to hold up in the air! Didn't Mr Blake make a fuss about us leaving that behind.
COLIN:	Yeah. He does go on. Anyway it was easy to get one from another of the students.
HELEN:	Now, the next section's the procedure. I sent you the draft of that.
COLIN:	Yeah. It was clear, but I don't think we need all these details of what time we left and what time we got back and how we divided up the different research tasks.
HELEN:	OK. I'll look at that again.
COLIN:	Then we have to describe our method of investigation in detail. So let's begin with how we measured wave speed. I was surprised how straightforward that was.
HELEN:	I'd expected us to have some sort of high-tech device, not just stand there and count the number of waves per minute. Not very precise, but I suppose it was good enough. But the way we measured the amount of salt was interesting.
COLIN:	In the water from the rock pools?
HELEN:	Yeah, oh, I wanted to check the chemicals we used in the lab when we analysed those samples – was it potassium chromate and silver nitrate?
COLIN:	That's right.
HELEN:	OK. And we need the map of the seashore. You just left that to me. And I had to do it while the tide was low, well that was OK, but the place I started it from was down on the beach, then I realised I should have gone up higher to get better visibility, so I had to start all over again. But at least I'd got the squared paper or I'd have had problems drawing it all to scale.
COLIN:	Yes. It looks good. We could get a map of the region off the internet and see if we need to make any changes.
HELEN:	I had a look but I couldn't find anything. But you took some pictures, didn't you?
COLIN:	Yeah. I'll email you them if you want.
HELEN:	OK. I'll make my amendments using those, then I can scan it into our report. Great.

Q22

Q23

Q24

Q25

Q26

HELEN:	Now when we get to our findings I thought we could divide them up into the different zones we identified on the shore and the problems organisms face in each zone. So for the highest area …
COLIN:	… the splash zone?
HELEN:	Yeah, we found mostly those tiny shellfish that have strong hard shells that act as protection.
COLIN:	But not from other organisms that might eat them, predators?
HELEN:	No, that's not the main danger for them. But the shells prevent them from drying out because they're in the open air for most of the time.
COLIN:	Right. And since they're exposed, they need to be able to find some sort of shelter, or cover themselves up, so they don't get too hot. Then in the middle and lower zones, nearer the sea, we need to discuss the effects of wave action …
HELEN:	Yes, and how organisms develop structures to prevent themselves from being swept away, or even destroyed by being smashed against the rocks.
COLIN:	I haven't done anything on the geological changes. I don't know what to put for that.
HELEN:	No, we weren't concentrating on that. Maybe we need to find some websites.
COLIN:	Good idea. I've got the lecture notes from Mr Blake's geology course, but they're too general. But we could ask him which books on our Reading List might be most helpful.

Q27 & 28

Q27 & 28

HELEN:	Right. OK, now I did a draft of the section of sources of possible error in our research, but I don't know if you agree. For example, the size of the sample, and whether it's big enough to make any general conclusions from. But I thought actually we did have quite a big sample.	
COLIN:	We did. And our general method of observation seemed quite reliable. But we might not be all that accurate as far as the actual numbers go.	
HELEN:	Yeah, <u>we might have missed some organisms – if they were hiding under a rock, for example</u>. I wasn't sure about the way we described their habitats. I decided it was probably OK.	*Q29 & 30*
COLIN:	Yeah, and the descriptions we gave of the smaller organisms, they weren't very detailed, but they were adequate in this context. <u>I'm not sure we identified all the species correctly though</u>.	*Q29 & 30*
HELEN:	OK, we'd better mention that. Now, how …	

SECTION 4

We've been discussing the factors the architect has to consider when designing domestic buildings. I'm going to move on now to consider the design of *public* buildings, and I'll illustrate this by referring to the new Taylor Concert Hall that's recently been completed here in the city.

So, as with a domestic building, when designing a public building, an architect needs to consider the function of the building – for example, is it to be used primarily for entertainment, or for education, or for administration? The second thing the architect needs to think about is the context of the building, <u>this includes its physical location, obviously, but it also includes the social meaning of the building, how it relates to the people it's built for</u>. And finally, for important public buildings, the architect may also be looking for a central symbolic idea on which to base the design, a sort of metaphor for the building and the way in which it is used. *Q31*

Let's look at the new Taylor Concert Hall in relation to these ideas. <u>The location chosen was a site in a run-down district that has been ignored in previous redevelopment plans. It was occupied by a factory that had been empty for some years</u>. The whole area was some distance from the high-rise office blocks of the central business district and shopping centre, but it was only one kilometre from the ring road. <u>The site itself was bordered to the north by a canal</u> which had once been used by boats bringing in raw materials when the area was used for manufacturing. *Q32* *Q33*

The architect chosen for the project was Tom Harrison. He found the main design challenge was the location of the site in an area that had no neighbouring buildings of any importance. To reflect the fact that the significance of the building in this quite run-down location was as yet unknown, he decided to create a building centred around the idea of a mystery – something whose meaning still has to be discovered.

So how was this reflected in the design of the building? Well, Harrison decided to create pedestrian access to the building and to make use of the presence of water on the site. <u>As people approach the entrance, they therefore have to cross over a bridge</u>. He wanted to give people a feeling of suspense as they see the building first from a distance, and then close-up, and <u>the initial impression he wanted to create from the shape of the building as a whole was that of a box</u>. The first side that people see, the southern wall, is just a high, flat wall uninterrupted by any windows. This might sound off-putting, but it supports Harrison's concept of the building – that the person approaching is intrigued and wonders what will be inside. <u>And this flat wall also has another purpose. At night-time, projectors are switched on and it functions as a huge screen, onto which images are projected</u>. *Q34* *Q35* *Q36*

The auditorium itself seats 1500 people. The floor's supported by ten massive pads.   *Q37*
These are constructed from rubber, and so are able to absorb any vibrations from outside
and prevent them from affecting the auditorium. The walls are made of several layers of
honey-coloured wood, all sourced from local beech trees. In order to improve the acoustic
properties of the auditorium and to amplify the sound, they are not straight, they are curved.   *Q38*
The acoustics are also adjustable according to the size of orchestra and the type of music
being played. In order to achieve this, there are nine movable panels in the ceiling above the
orchestra which are all individually motorized, and the walls also have curtains which can be   *Q39*
opened or closed to change the acoustics.

The reaction of the public to the new building has generally been positive. However, the   *Q40*
evaluation of some critics has been less enthusiastic. In spite of Harrison's efforts to use local
materials, they criticise the style of the design as being international rather than local, and
say it doesn't reflect features of the landscape or society for which it is built.

TEST 3

SECTION 1

MARTIN: Good morning. This is Burnham tourist office, Martin speaking.

SUE: Oh, hello. I saw a poster about free things to do in the area, and it said people should
phone you for information. I'm coming to Burnham with my husband and two children
for a few days on June the 27th, or possibly the 28th, and I'd like some ideas for   *Example*
things to do on the 29th.

MARTIN: Yes, of course. OK. Then let's start with a couple of events especially for children.
The art gallery is holding an event called 'Family Welcome' that day, when there are
activities and trails to use throughout the gallery.

SUE: That sounds interesting. What time does it start?

MARTIN: The gallery opens at 10, and the 'Family Welcome' event runs from 10.30 until 2   *Q1*
o'clock. The gallery stays open until 5. And several times during the day, they're   *Q2*
going to show a short film that the gallery has produced. It demonstrates how
ceramics are made, and there'll be equipment and materials for children to have a go
themselves. Last time they ran the event, there was a film about painting, which went
down very well with the children, and they're now working on one about sculpture.

SUE: I like the sound of that. And what other events happen in Burnham?

MARTIN: Well, do you all enjoy listening to music?

SUE: Oh, yes.

MARTIN: Well there are several free concerts taking place at different times – one or two in the
morning, the majority at lunchtime, and a couple in the evening. And they range from   *Q3*
pop music to Latin American.

SUE: The Latin American could be fun. What time is that?

MARTIN: It's being repeated several times, in different places. They're performing in the central
library at 1 o'clock, then at 4 it's in the City Museum, and in the evening, at 7.30,   *Q4*
there's a longer concert, in the theatre.

SUE: Right. I'll suggest that to the rest of the family.

MARTIN: Something else you might be interested in is the boat race along the river.

SUE: Oh, yes, do tell me about that.

MARTIN: The race starts at Offord Marina, to the north of Burnham, and goes as far as   *Q5*
Summer Pool. The best place to watch it from is Charlesworth Bridge, though that
does get rather crowded.

SUE:	And who's taking part?	
MARTIN:	Well, local boat clubs, but the standard is very high. <u>One of them came first in the West</u> <u>of England regional championship in May this year</u> – it was the first time a team from Burnham has won. It means that next year they'll be representing the region in the national championship.	Q6

SUE:	Now I've heard something about Paxton Nature Reserve. <u>It's a good place for spotting unusual</u> <u>birds, isn't it?</u>	Q7
MARTIN:	<u>That's right – throughout the year</u>. There is a lake there, as well as a river, and they provide a very attractive habitat. So it's a good idea to bring binoculars if you have them. <u>And just at</u> <u>the moment you can see various flowers that are pretty unusual</u> – the soil at Paxton isn't very common. They're looking good right now.	Q8
SUE:	Right. My husband will be particularly interested in that.	
MARTIN:	<u>And there's going to be a talk and slide show about mushrooms – and you'll be able to go out</u> <u>and pick some afterwards and study the different varieties.</u>	Q9
SUE:	Uhuh. And is it possible for children to swim in the river?	
MARTIN:	Yes. <u>Part of it has been fenced off to make it safe for children to swim in</u>. It's very shallow, and there's a lifeguard on duty whenever it's open. The lake is too deep, so swimming isn't allowed there.	Q10
SUE:	OK, we must remember to bring their swimming things, in case we go to Paxton. How long does it take to get there by car from Burnham?	
MARTIN:	About 20 minutes, but parking is very limited, so it's usually much easier to go by bus – and it takes about the same time.	
SUE:	Right. Well, I'll discuss the options with the rest of the family. Thanks very much for all your help.	
MARTIN:	You're welcome.	
SUE:	Goodbye.	
MARTIN:	Bye.	

SECTION 2

MAN:	First of all, let me thank you all for coming to this public meeting, to discuss the future of our town. Our first speaker is Shona Ferguson, from Barford town council. Shona.	
SHONA:	Thank you. First I'll briefly give you some background information, then I'll be asking you for your comments on developments in the town.	
	Well, as you don't need me to tell you, Barford has changed a great deal in the last 50 years. These are some of the main changes.	
	Fifty years ago, buses linked virtually every part of the town and the neighbouring towns and villages. Most people used them frequently, <u>but not now, because the bus companies</u> <u>concentrate on just the routes that attract most passengers. So parts of the town are no longer</u> <u>served by buses</u>. Even replacing old uncomfortable buses with smart new ones has had little impact on passenger numbers. It's sometimes said that bus fares are too high, but in relation to average incomes, fares are not much higher than they were 50 years ago.	Q11
	Changes in the road network are affecting the town. The centre was recently closed to traffic on a trial basis, making it much safer for pedestrians. The impact of this is being measured. <u>The</u> <u>new cycle paths, separating bikes from cars in most main roads, are being used far more than</u> <u>was expected, reducing traffic and improving air quality</u>. And although the council's attempts to have a bypass constructed have failed, we haven't given up hope of persuading the government to change its mind.	Q12
	Shopping in the town centre has changed over the years. Many of us can remember when the town was crowded with people going shopping. Numbers have been falling for several years, despite efforts to attract shoppers, for instance by opening new car parks. Some people combine	

shopping with visits to the town's restaurants and cafés. Most shops are small independent stores, which is good, but many people prefer to use supermarkets and department stores in nearby large towns, as there are so few well-known chain stores here.   Q13

Turning now to medical facilities, the town is served by family doctors in several medical practices – fewer than 50 years ago, but each catering for far more patients. Our hospital closed 15 years ago, which means journeys to other towns are unavoidable. On the other hand, there are more dentists than there used to be.   Q14

Employment patterns have changed, along with almost everything else. The number of schools and colleges has increased, making that the main employment sector. Services, such as website design and accountancy, have grown in importance, and surprisingly, perhaps, manufacturing hasn't seen the decline that has affected it in other parts of the country.   Q15

Now I'll very quickly outline current plans for some of the town's facilities, before asking for your comments.

As you'll know if you regularly use the car park at the railway station, it's usually full. The railway company applied for permission to replace it with a multi-storey car park, but that was refused. Instead, the company has bought some adjoining land, and this will be used to increase the number of parking spaces.   Q16

The Grand, the old cinema in the high street, will close at the end of the year, and reopen on a different site. You've probably seen the building under construction. The plan is to have three screens with fewer seats, rather than just the one large auditorium in the old cinema.   Q17

I expect many of you shop in the indoor market. It's become more and more shabby-looking, and because of fears about safety, it was threatened with demolition. The good news is that it will close for six weeks to be made safe and redecorated, and the improved building will open in July.   Q18

Lots of people use the library, including school and college students who go there to study. The council has managed to secure funding to keep the library open later into the evening, twice a week. We would like to enlarge the building in the not-too-distant future, but this is by no means definite.   Q19

There's no limit on access to the nature reserve on the edge of town, and this will continue to be the case. What *will* change, though, is that the council will no longer be in charge of the area. Instead it will become the responsibility of a national body that administers most nature reserves in the country.   Q20

OK, now let me ask you …

SECTION 3

JEREMY: Hello, Helen. Sorry I'm late.

HELEN: Hi, Jeremy, no problem. Well we'd better work out where we are on our project, I suppose.

JEREMY: Yeah. I've looked at the drawings you've done for my story, 'The Forest', and I think they're brilliant – they really create the atmosphere I had in mind when I was writing it.

HELEN: I'm glad you like them.

JEREMY: There are just a few suggestions I'd like to make.

HELEN: Go ahead.

JEREMY: Now, I'm not sure about the drawing of the cave – it's got trees all around it, which is   Q21
great, but the drawing's a bit too static, isn't it? I think it needs some action.

HELEN:	Yes, there's nothing happening. Perhaps I should add the boy – Malcolm, isn't it? He would be walking up to it.
JEREMY:	Yes, let's have Malcolm in the drawing. And what about putting in a tiger – the one that he makes friends with a bit later? Maybe it could be sitting under a tree washing itself.
HELEN:	And the tiger stops in the middle of what it's doing when it sees Malcolm walking past.
JEREMY:	That's a good idea.
HELEN:	OK, I'll have a go at that.
JEREMY:	Then there's the drawing of the crowd of men and women dancing. They're just outside the forest, and there's a lot going on.
HELEN:	That's right, you wanted them to be watching a carnival procession, but I thought it would be too crowded. Do you think it works like this?
JEREMY:	Yes, I like what you've done. The only thing is, could you add Malcolm to it, without changing what's already there.
HELEN:	What about having him sitting on the tree trunk on the right of the picture?
JEREMY:	Yes, that would be fine.
HELEN:	And do you want him watching the other people?
JEREMY:	No, he's been left out of all the fun, so I'd like him to be crying – that'll contrast nicely with the next picture, where he's laughing at the clowns in the carnival.
HELEN:	Right, I'll do that.
JEREMY:	And then the drawing of the people ice skating in the forest.
HELEN:	I wasn't too happy with that one. Because they're supposed to be skating on grass, aren't they?
JEREMY:	That's right, and it's frozen over. At the moment it doesn't look quite right.
HELEN:	Mm, I see what you mean. I'll have another go at that.
JEREMY:	And I like the wool hats they're wearing. Maybe you could give each of them a scarf, as well.
HELEN:	Yeah, that's easy enough. They can be streaming out behind the people to suggest they're skating really fast.
JEREMY:	Mm, great. Well that's all on the drawings.
HELEN:	Right. So you've finished writing your story and I just need to finish illustrating it, and my story and your drawings are done.

Q22

Q23

Q24

Q25

Q26

HELEN:	So the next thing is to decide what exactly we need to write about in the report that goes with the stories, and how we're going to divide the work.
JEREMY:	Right, Helen.
HELEN:	What do you think about including a section on how we planned the project as a whole, Jeremy? That's probably quite important.
JEREMY:	Yeah. Well, you've had most of the good ideas so far. How do you feel about drafting something, then we can go through it together and discuss it?
HELEN:	OK, that seems reasonable. And I could include something on how we came up with the ideas for our two stories, couldn't I?
JEREMY:	Well I've started writing something about that, so why don't you do the same and we can include the two things.
HELEN:	Right. So what about our interpretation of the stories? Do we need to write about what we think they show, like the value of helping other people, all that sort of thing?
JEREMY:	That's going to come up later, isn't it? I think everyone in the class is going to read each other's stories and come up with their own interpretations, which we're going to discuss.
HELEN:	Oh, I missed that. So it isn't going to be part of the report at all?

Q27

Q28

Q29

JEREMY: No. But we need to write about the illustrations, because they're an essential
          element of children's experience of reading the stories. It's probably easiest for you
          to write that section, as you know more about drawing than I do.

HELEN: Maybe, but I find it quite hard to write about. <u>I'd be happier if you did it.</u>   Q30

JEREMY: OK. So when do you think …

SECTION 4

So what I'm going to talk about to you today is something called Ethnography. This is a type
of research aimed at exploring the way human cultures work. It was first developed for use in
anthropology, and it's also been used in sociology and communication studies. So what's it
got to do with business, you may ask. Well, businesses are finding that <u>ethnography can offer</u>   Q31
<u>them deeper insight into the possible needs of customers, either present or future, as well as</u>
<u>providing valuable information about their attitudes towards existing products</u>. And ethnography
can also help companies to design new products or services that customers really want.

Let's look at some examples of how ethnographic research works in business. One team of
researchers did a project for a company manufacturing kitchen equipment. They watched
how cooks used measuring cups to measure out things like sugar and flour. They saw that
the cooks had to check and recheck the contents, because <u>although the measuring cups</u>   Q32
<u>had numbers</u> inside them, <u>the cooks couldn't see these easily</u>. So a new design of cup was
developed to overcome this problem, and it was a top seller.

Another team of ethnographic researchers looked at how cell phones were used in Uganda,
in Africa. They found that people who didn't have their own phones could pay to use the
phones of local entrepreneurs. Because these customers paid in advance for their calls, <u>they</u>   Q33
<u>were eager to know how much time they'd spent on the call so far</u>. So the phone company
designed phones for use globally with this added feature.

Ethnographic research has also been carried out in computer companies. In one company, IT
systems administrators were observed for several weeks. It was found that a large amount of
their work involved communicating with colleagues in order to solve problems, but that <u>they</u>   Q34
<u>didn't have a standard way of exchanging information from spreadsheets and so on. So the</u>
<u>team came up with an idea for software that would help them to do this</u>.

In another piece of research, a team observed and talked to nurses working in hospitals.
<u>This led to the recognition that the nurses needed to access the computer records of their</u>   Q35
<u>patients, no matter where they were</u>. This led to the development of a portable computer
tablet that allowed the nurses to check records in locations throughout the hospital.

Occasionally, research can be done even in environments where the researchers can't be
present. For example, in one project done for an airline, <u>respondents used their smartphones</u>   Q36
<u>to record information during airline trips, in a study aiming at tracking the emotions of</u>
<u>passengers during a flight</u>.

So what makes studies like these different from ordinary research? Let's look at some of the
general principles behind ethnographic research in business. First of all, the researcher has to
be completely open-minded – he or she hasn't thought up a hypothesis to be tested, as is the
case in other types of research. Instead they wait for the participants in the research to inform
them. As far as choosing the participants themselves is concerned, that's not really all that
different from ordinary research – the criteria according to which the participants are chosen
may be something as simple as the age bracket they fall into, <u>or the researchers may select</u>   Q37
<u>them according to their income</u>, or they might try to find a set of people who all use a particular

product, for example. But it's absolutely crucial to recruit the right people as participants. As well as the criteria I've mentioned, <u>they have to be comfortable talking about themselves and being watched as they go about their activities</u>. Actually, most researchers say that people open up pretty easily, maybe because they're often in their own home or workplace.

So what makes this type of research special is that it's not just a matter of sending a questionnaire to the participants, instead <u>the research is usually based on first-hand observation of what they are doing at the time</u>. But that doesn't mean that the researcher never talks to the participants. However, unlike in traditional research, in this case it's the participant rather than the researchers who decides what direction the interview will follow. This means that there's less likelihood of the researcher imposing his or her own ideas on the participant.

But after they've said goodbye to their participants and got back to their office, the researchers' work isn't finished. <u>Most researchers estimate that 70 to 80 per cent of their time is spent not on the collecting of data but on its analysis – looking at photos, listening to recordings and transcribing them, and so on</u>. The researchers may end up with hundreds of pages of notes. And to determine what's significant, they don't focus on the sensational things or the unusual things, instead they try to identify a pattern of some sort in all this data, and to discern the meaning behind it. This can result in some compelling insights that can in turn feed back to the whole design process.

TEST 4

SECTION 1

ROB: Good morning. Stretton Festival box office. How can I help you?

MELANIE: Oh, hello. My family and I are on holiday in the area, and we've seen some posters about the festival this week. Could you tell me about some of the events, please?

ROB: Of course.

MELANIE: First of all, are there still tickets available for the jazz band on Saturday?

ROB: There are, but only £15. The £12 seats have all been sold.   *Example*

MELANIE: OK. And the venue is the school, isn't it?

ROB: Yes, that's right, <u>the secondary school</u>. Make sure you don't go to the primary school   *Q1*
           by mistake! And there's an additional performer who isn't mentioned on the posters
           – Carolyn Hart is going to play with the band.

MELANIE: Oh, I think I've heard her on the radio. Doesn't she play the oboe, or flute or
           something?

ROB: <u>Yes, the flute.</u> She usually plays with symphony orchestras, and apparently this is   *Q2*
           her first time with a jazz band.

MELANIE: Well, I'd certainly like to hear *her*. Then the next thing I want to ask about is the duck
           races – I saw a poster beside a river. What are they, exactly?

ROB: Well, you buy a yellow plastic duck – or as many as you like – they're a pound each.
           And you write your name on each one. There'll be several races, depending on the
           number of ducks taking part. And John Stevens, a champion swimmer who lives
           locally, is going to start the races. <u>All the ducks will be launched into the river at the</u>   *Q3*
           <u>back of the cinema</u>, then they'll float along the river for 500 metres, as far as the
           railway bridge.

MELANIE: And are there any prizes?

ROB:	Yes, <u>the first duck in each race to arrive at the finishing line wins its owner free tickets for the concert on the last night of the festival</u>.	*Q4*
MELANIE:	You said you can buy a duck? I'm sure my children will both want one.	
ROB:	<u>They're on sale at a stall in the market</u>. You can't miss it – it's got an enormous sign showing a couple of ducks.	*Q5*
MELANIE:	OK. I'll go there this afternoon. I remember walking past there yesterday. Now could you tell me something about the flower show, please?	
ROB:	Well, admission is free, and the show is being held in <u>Bythwaite</u> Hall.	*Q6*
MELANIE:	Sorry, how do you spell that?	
ROB:	B-Y-T-H-W-A-I-T-E. Bythwaite.	
MELANIE:	Is it easy to find? I'm not very familiar with the town yet.	
ROB:	Oh, you won't have any problem. It's right in the centre of Stretton. It's the only old building in the town, so it's easy to recognise.	
MELANIE:	I know it. I presume it's open all day.	
ROB:	Yes, but if you'd like to see the prizes being awarded for the best flowers, you'll need to be there at 5 o'clock. <u>The prizes are being given by a famous actor, Kevin Shapless</u>. He lives nearby and gets involved in a lot of community events.	*Q7*
MELANIE:	Gosh, I've seen him on TV. I'll definitely go to the prize-giving.	
ROB:	Right.	

MELANIE:	I've seen a list of plays that are being performed this week, and I'd like to know which are suitable for my children, and which ones my husband and I might go to.	
ROB:	How old are your children?	
MELANIE:	Five and seven. What about 'The Mystery of Muldoon'?	
ROB:	<u>That's aimed at five to ten-year-olds</u>.	*Q8*
MELANIE:	So if I take my children, I can expect them to enjoy it more than I do?	
ROB:	I think so. <u>If you'd like something for yourself and your husband, and leave your children with a babysitter, you might like to see 'Fire and Flood'</u> – it's about events that really happened in Stretton two hundred years ago, and children might find it rather frightening.	*Q9*
MELANIE:	Oh, thanks for the warning. And finally, what about 'Silly Sailor'?	
ROB:	That's a comedy, and <u>it's for young and old</u>. In fact, it won an award in the Stretton Drama Festival a couple of months ago.	*Q10*
MELANIE:	OK. Well, goodbye, and thanks for all the information. I'm looking forward to the festival!	
ROB:	Goodbye.	

SECTION 2

Good morning, and welcome to the museum – one with a remarkable range of exhibits, which I'm sure you'll enjoy. My name's Greg, and I'll tell you about the various collections as we go round. But before we go, let me just give you a taste of what we have here.

Well, for one thing, we have a fine collection of twentieth and twenty-first century paintings, many by very well-known artists. I'm sure you'll recognise several of the paintings. <u>This is the gallery that attracts the largest number of visitors</u>, so it's best to go in early in the day, before the crowds arrive. *Q11*

Then there are the nineteenth-century paintings. The museum was opened in the middle of that century, and <u>several of the artists each donated one work</u> – to get the museum started, as it were. So they're of special interest to us – we feel closer to them than to other works. *Q12*

The sculpture gallery has a number of fine exhibits, but I'm afraid it's currently closed for refurbishment. You'll need to come back next year to see it properly, but <u>a number of the sculptures have been moved to other parts of the museum</u>.   Q13

<u>'Around the world' is a temporary exhibition – you've probably seen something about it on TV or in the newspapers</u>. It's created a great deal of interest, because it presents objects from every continent and many countries, and provides information about their social context – why they were made, who for, and so on.   Q14

Then there's the collection of coins. This is what you might call a focused, specialist collection, because all the coins come from this country, and were produced between two thousand and a thousand years ago. <u>And many of them were discovered by ordinary people digging their gardens, and donated to the museum!</u>   Q15

<u>All our porcelain and glass was left to the museum by its founder</u>, when he died in 1878. And in the terms of his will, we're not allowed to add anything to that collection: he believed it was perfect in itself, and we don't see any reason to disagree!   Q16

OK, that was something about the collections, and now here's some more practical information, in case you need it. Most of the museum facilities are downstairs, in the basement, so you go down the stairs here. When you reach the bottom of the stairs, you'll find yourself in a sitting area, with comfortable chairs and sofas where you can have a rest before continuing your exploration of the museum.

We have a very good restaurant, which serves excellent food all day, in a relaxing atmosphere. <u>To reach it, when you get to the bottom of the stairs, go straight ahead to the far side of the sitting area, then turn right into the corridor. You'll see the door of the restaurant facing you</u>.   Q17

If you just want a snack, or if you'd like to eat somewhere with facilities for children, we also have a café. <u>When you reach the bottom of the stairs, you'll need to go straight ahead, turn right into the corridor, and the café is immediately on the right</u>.   Q18

And talking about children, <u>there are baby-changing facilities downstairs: cross the sitting area, continue straight ahead along the corridor on the left, and you and your baby will find the facilities on the left-hand side</u>.   Q19

<u>The cloakroom, where you should leave coats, umbrellas and any large bags, is on the left hand side of the sitting area. It's through the last door before you come to the corridor</u>.   Q20

There are toilets on every floor, but in the basement they're the first rooms on the left when you get down there.

OK, now if you've got anything to leave in the cloakroom, please do that now, and then we'll start our tour.

SECTION 3

SUPERVISOR: Hi, Joanna, good to meet you. Now, before we discuss your new research project, I'd like to hear something about the psychology study you did last year for your Master's degree. So how did you choose your subjects for that?

JOANNA: Well, I had six subjects, all professional musicians, and all female. Three were violinists and there was also a cello player and a pianist and a flute player. They were all very highly regarded in the music world and <u>they'd done quite extensive tours in different continents</u>, and quite a few had won prizes and competitions as well.   Q21 & 22

SUPERVISOR:	And they were quite young, weren't they?	
JOANNA:	Yes, between 25 and 29 – the mean was 27.8. <u>I wasn't specifically looking for artists who'd produced recordings, but this is something that's just taken for granted these days, and they all had.</u>	*Q21 & 22*
SUPERVISOR:	Right. Now you collected your data through telephone interviews, didn't you?	
JOANNA:	Yes. <u>I realised if I was going to interview leading musicians it'd only be possible over the phone because they're so busy.</u> I recorded them using a telephone recording adaptor. I'd been worried about the quality, but it worked out all right. I managed at least a 30-minute interview with each subject, sometimes longer.	*Q23 & 24*
SUPERVISOR:	Did doing it on the phone make it more stressful?	
JOANNA:	I'd thought it might … it was all quite informal though and in fact they seemed very keen to talk. <u>And I don't think using the phone meant I got less rich data, rather the opposite in fact.</u>	*Q23 & 24*
SUPERVISOR:	Interesting. And you were looking at how performers dress for concert performances?	
JOANNA:	That's right. My research investigated the way players see their role as a musician and how this is linked to the type of clothing they decide to wear. But that focus didn't emerge immediately. <u>When I started I was more interested in trying to investigate the impact of what was worn on those listening,</u> and also <u>whether someone like a violinist might adopt a different style of clothing from, say, someone playing the flute or the trumpet.</u>	*Q25 & 26* *Q25 & 26*
SUPERVISOR:	It's interesting that the choice of dress is up to the individual, isn't it?	
JOANNA:	Yes, you'd expect there to be rules about it in orchestras, but that's quite rare.	

SUPERVISOR:	You only had women performers in your study. Was that because male musicians are less worried about fashion?	
JOANNA:	I think a lot of the men are very much influenced by fashion, but <u>in social terms the choices they have are more limited … they'd really upset audiences if they strayed away from quite narrow boundaries.</u>	*Q27*
SUPERVISOR:	Hmm. Now, popular music has quite different expectations. Did you read Mike Frost's article about the dress of women performers in popular music?	
JOANNA:	No.	
SUPERVISOR:	He points out that a lot of female singers and musicians in popular music tend to dress down in performances, and wear less feminine clothes, like jeans instead of skirts, and <u>he suggests this is because otherwise they'd just be discounted as trivial.</u>	*Q28*
JOANNA:	But you could argue they're just wearing what's practical … I mean, a pop-music concert is usually a pretty energetic affair.	
SUPERVISOR:	Yes, he doesn't make that point, but I think you're probably right. I was interested by the effect of the audience at a musical performance when it came to the choice of dress.	
JOANNA:	The subjects I interviewed felt this was really important. It's all to do with what we understand by performance as a public event. <u>They believed the audience had certain expectations and it was up to them as performers to fulfil these expectations, to show a kind of esteem</u> …	*Q29*
SUPERVISOR:	… they weren't afraid of looking as if they'd made an effort to look good.	
JOANNA:	Mmm. I think in the past the audience would have had those expectations of one another too, but that's not really the case now, not in the UK anyway.	
SUPERVISOR:	No.	
JOANNA:	And I also got interested in what sports scientists are doing too, with regard to clothing.	

SUPERVISOR:	Musicians are quite vulnerable physically, aren't they, because the movements they carry out are very intensive and repetitive, so <u>I'd imagine some features</u> <u>of sports clothing could safeguard the players from the potentially dangerous</u> <u>effects of this sort of thing.</u>	Q30
JOANNA:	Yes, but musicians don't really consider it. They avoid clothing that obviously restricts their movements, but that's as far as they go.	
SUPERVISOR:	Anyway, coming back to your own research, do you have any idea where you're going from here?	
JOANNA:	I was thinking of doing a study using an audience, including …	

SECTION 4

As we saw in the last lecture, a major cause of climate change is the rapid rise in the level of carbon dioxide in the atmosphere over the last century. If we could reduce the amount of CO_2, perhaps the rate of climate change could also be slowed down. One potential method involves enhancing the role of the soil that plants grow in, with regard to absorbing CO_2. Rattan Lal, a soil scientist from Ohio State University, in the USA, claims that the world's agricultural soils could potentially absorb 13 per cent of the carbon dioxide in the atmosphere – the equivalent of the amount released in the last 30 years. And research is going on into how this might be achieved.

Lal first came to the idea that soil might be valuable in this way not through an interest in climate change, but rather out of concern for the land itself and the people dependent on it. Carbon-rich soil is dark, crumbly and fertile, and retains some water. But <u>erosion can occur</u> **Q31** <u>if soil is dry</u>, which is a likely effect if it contains inadequate amounts of carbon. Erosion is of course bad for people trying to grow crops or breed animals on that terrain. In the 1970s and '80s, <u>Lal was studying soils in Africa so devoid of organic matter that the ground had</u> **Q32** <u>become extremely hard</u>, like cement. There he met a pioneer in the study of global warming, who suggested that carbon from the soil had moved into the atmosphere. This is now looking increasingly likely.

Let me explain. For millions of years, carbon dioxide levels in the atmosphere have been regulated, in part, by a natural partnership between plants and microbes – tiny organisms in the soil. <u>Plants absorb CO_2 from the air and transform it into sugars and other carbon-based</u> **Q33** <u>substances</u>. While a proportion of these carbon products remain in the plant, <u>some transfer</u> **Q34** <u>from the roots to fungi and soil microbes</u>, which store the carbon in the soil.

The invention of agriculture some 10,000 years ago disrupted these ancient soil-building processes and led to the loss of carbon from the soil. When humans started draining the natural topsoil, and ploughing it up for planting, they exposed the buried carbon to oxygen. This created carbon dioxide and released it into the air. And in some places, grazing by domesticated animals has removed all vegetation, releasing carbon into the air. Tons of carbon have been stripped from the world's soils – where it's needed – and pumped into the atmosphere.

So what can be done? Researchers are now coming up with evidence that even modest changes to farming can significantly help to reduce the amount of carbon in the atmosphere.

Some growers have already started using an approach known as regenerative agriculture. <u>This aims to boost the fertility of soil and keep it moist through established practices</u>. These **Q35** include keeping fields planted all year round, and <u>increasing the variety of plants being</u> **Q36** <u>grown</u>. Strategies like these can significantly increase the amount of carbon stored in the soil, so agricultural researchers are now building a case for their use in combating climate change.

One American investigation into the potential for storing CO_2 on agricultural lands is taking place in California. Soil scientist Whendee Silver of the University of California, Berkeley, is conducting a first-of-its-kind study on a large cattle farm in the state. She and her students *Q37* are testing the effects on carbon storage of the compost that is created from waste – both agricultural, including manure and cornstalks, and waste produced in gardens, such as *Q38* leaves, branches, and lawn trimmings.

In Australia, soil ecologist Christine Jones is testing another promising soil-enrichment strategy. Jones and 12 farmers are working to build up soil carbon by cultivating grasses *Q39* that stay green all year round. Like composting, the approach has already been proved experimentally; Jones now hopes to show that it can be applied on working farms and that the resulting carbon capture can be accurately measured.

It's hoped in the future that projects such as these will demonstrate the role that farmers and other land managers can play in reducing the harmful effects of greenhouse gases. For example, in countries like the United States, where most farming operations use large applications of fertiliser, changing such long-standing habits will require a change of system. Rattan Lal argues that farmers should receive payment not just for the corn or beef they *Q40* produce, but also for the carbon they can store in their soil.

Another study being carried out …

Listening and Reading Answer Keys

TEST 1

LISTENING

Section 1, Questions 1–10

1 Charlton
2 (£)115 / a/one hundred (and) fifteen
3 cash
4 parking
5 music
6 entry
7 stage
8 code
9 floor/floors
10 decoration/decorations

Section 2, Questions 11–20

11 animal/animals
12 tool/tools
13 shoes
14 dog/dogs
15 F
16 G
17 D
18 H
19 C
20 A

Section 3, Questions 21–30

21 C
22 B
23 B
24 C
25 A
26 B
27 C
28 A
29 B
30 A

Section 4, Questions 31–40

31 conservation
32 food/foods
33 surface
34 oxygen/O_2
35 mammals
36 ice
37 decline/declining/decrease
38 map
39 migration
40 consumption

If you score …

0–14	15–28	29–40
you are unlikely to get an acceptable score under examination conditions and we recommend that you spend a lot of time improving your English before you take IELTS.	you may get an acceptable score under examination conditions but we recommend that you think about having more practice or lessons before you take IELTS.	you are likely to get an acceptable score under examination conditions but remember that different institutions will find different scores acceptable.

READING

Reading Passage 1, Questions 1–13

1   tomatoes
2   urban centres/centers
3   energy
4   fossil fuel
5   artificial
6   (stacked) trays
7   (urban) rooftops
8   NOT GIVEN
9   TRUE
10   FALSE
11   TRUE
12   FALSE
13   TRUE

Reading Passage 2, Questions 14–26

14   FALSE
15   NOT GIVEN
16   TRUE
17   NOT GIVEN
18   FALSE
19   TRUE
20   gates
21   clamp
22   axle
23   cogs
24   aqueduct
25   wall
26   locks

Reading Passage 3, Questions 27–40

27   D
28   B
29   A
30   sunshade
31   iron
32   algae
33   clouds
34   cables
35   snow
36   rivers
37   B
38   D
39   C
40   A

If you score ...

0–11	12–24	25–40
you are unlikely to get an acceptable score under examination conditions and we recommend that you spend a lot of time improving your English before you take IELTS.	you may get an acceptable score under examination conditions but we recommend that you think about having more practice or lessons before you take IELTS.	you are likely to get an acceptable score under examination conditions but remember that different institutions will find different scores acceptable.

TEST 2

LISTENING

Section 1, Questions 1–10

1 hostel
2 Buckleigh
3 PE9 7QT
4 waiter
5 politics
6 cycling
7 cinema
8 disabled
9 4.30 (pm) / half past four
10 07788 136711

Section 2, Questions 11–20

11&12 *IN EITHER ORDER*
    A
    B
13&14 *IN EITHER ORDER*
    B
    D
15&16 *IN EITHER ORDER*
    C
    E
17 G
18 D
19 B
20 F

Section 3, Questions 21–30

21 A
22 A
23 C
24 B
25 B
26 B
27&28 *IN EITHER ORDER*
    A
    D
29&30 *IN EITHER ORDER*
    C
    E

Section 4, Questions 31–40

31 social
32 factory
33 canal
34 bridge
35 box
36 screen
37 rubber
38 curved
39 curtains
40 international

If you score …

0–14	15–28	29–40
you are unlikely to get an acceptable score under examination conditions and we recommend that you spend a lot of time improving your English before you take IELTS.	you may get an acceptable score under examination conditions but we recommend that you think about having more practice or lessons before you take IELTS.	you are likely to get an acceptable score under examination conditions but remember that different institutions will find different scores acceptable.

READING

Reading Passage 1, Questions 1–13

1 TRUE
2 NOT GIVEN
3 TRUE
4 FALSE
5 C
6 B
7 G
8 A
9 (lifting) frame
10 hydraulic jacks
11 stabbing guides
12 (lifting) cradle
13 air bags

Reading Passage 2, Questions 14–26

14 ii
15 ix
16 viii
17 i
18 iv
19 vii
20 vi
21 farming
22 canoes
23 birds
24 wood
25&26 *IN EITHER ORDER*
    B
    C

Reading Passage 3, Questions 27–40

27 C
28 D
29 B
30 A
31 C
32 B
33 H
34 NOT GIVEN
35 YES
36 NO
37 NO
38 YES
39 NOT GIVEN
40 A

If you score …

0–11	12–24	25–40
you are unlikely to get an acceptable score under examination conditions and we recommend that you spend a lot of time improving your English before you take IELTS.	you may get an acceptable score under examination conditions but we recommend that you think about having more practice or lessons before you take IELTS.	you are likely to get an acceptable score under examination conditions but remember that different institutions will find different scores acceptable.

TEST 3

LISTENING

Section 1, Questions 1–10

1	B
2	C
3	B
4	A
5	C
6	A
7	birds
8	flowers
9	mushrooms
10	river

Section 2, Questions 11–20

11	C
12	B
13	B
14	A
15	C
16	G
17	A
18	C
19	B
20	F

Section 3, Questions 21–30

21	cave
22	tiger
23	dancing
24	crying
25	grass
26	scarf
27	A
28	C
29	D
30	B

Section 4, Questions 31–40

31	attitude/attitudes
32	numbers
33	time/minutes
34	software
35	patients
36	emotions/feelings
37	income
38	comfortable
39	observation
40	analysis

If you score ...

0–14	15–30	31–40
you are unlikely to get an acceptable score under examination conditions and we recommend that you spend a lot of time improving your English before you take IELTS.	you may get an acceptable score under examination conditions but we recommend that you think about having more practice or lessons before you take IELTS.	you are likely to get an acceptable score under examination conditions but remember that different institutions will find different scores acceptable.

READING

Reading Passage 1, Questions 1–13

1 tea
2 reel
3 women
4 royalty
5 currency
6 paper
7 wool
8 monks
9 nylon
10 FALSE
11 TRUE
12 FALSE
13 NOT GIVEN

Reading Passage 2, Questions 14–26

14 FALSE
15 TRUE
16 NOT GIVEN
17 TRUE
18 FALSE
19 G
20 C
21 A
22 E
23 speed
24 plains
25 bottlenecks
26 corridor/passageway

Reading Passage 3, Questions 27–40

27 D
28 B
29 G
30 C
31 B
32 E
33 A
34 F
35 beginner
36 arithmetic
37 intuitive
38 scientists
39 experiments
40 theorems

If you score …

0–12	13–25	26–40
you are unlikely to get an acceptable score under examination conditions and we recommend that you spend a lot of time improving your English before you take IELTS.	you may get an acceptable score under examination conditions but we recommend that you think about having more practice or lessons before you take IELTS.	you are likely to get an acceptable score under examination conditions but remember that different institutions will find different scores acceptable.

TEST 4

LISTENING

Section 1, Questions 1–10

1	secondary
2	flute
3	cinema
4	concert
5	market
6	Bythwaite
7	actor
8	A
9	B
10	C

Section 2, Questions 11–20

11	E
12	D
13	G
14	B
15	C
16	A
17	F
18	H
19	C
20	B

Section 3, Questions 21–30

21&22	**IN EITHER ORDER**
	B
	D
23&24	**IN EITHER ORDER**
	A
	B
25&26	**IN EITHER ORDER**
	B
	E
27	C
28	A
29	A
30	C

Section 4, Questions 31–40

31	dry
32	hard
33	sugar/sugars
34	roots
35	moist/damp/wet
36	variety
37	cattle
38	gardens/gardening
39	grasses
40	payment/payments / money

If you score ...

0–14	15–28	29–40
you are unlikely to get an acceptable score under examination conditions and we recommend that you spend a lot of time improving your English before you take IELTS.	you may get an acceptable score under examination conditions but we recommend that you think about having more practice or lessons before you take IELTS.	you are likely to get an acceptable score under examination conditions but remember that different institutions will find different scores acceptable.

READING

Reading Passage 1,
Questions 1–13

1   FALSE
2   NOT GIVEN
3   NOT GIVEN
4   TRUE
5   A
6   C
7   B
8   A
9   A
10 D
11 B
12 E
13 F

Reading Passage 2,
Questions 14–26

14 B
15 A
16 B
17 D
18 C
19 D
20 TRUE
21 TRUE
22 NOT GIVEN
23 TRUE
24 FALSE
25 C
26 A

Reading Passage 3,
Questions 27–40

27 vi
28 iv
29 ii
30 vii
31 i
32 v
33 E
34 G
35 B
36 F
37 NO
38 YES
39 NOT GIVEN
40 YES

If you score ...

0–12	13–25	26–40
you are unlikely to get an acceptable score under examination conditions and we recommend that you spend a lot of time improving your English before you take IELTS.	you may get an acceptable score under examination conditions but we recommend that you think about having more practice or lessons before you take IELTS.	you are likely to get an acceptable score under examination conditions but remember that different institutions will find different scores acceptable.

Sample answers for Writing tasks

TEST 1, WRITING TASK 1

SAMPLE ANSWER

This is an answer written by a candidate who achieved a **Band 4.5** score. Here is the examiner's comment:

> The candidate covers all the data in the charts, but there is some inaccuracy in his description (*the largest percentage went with the Agricultural and farms*) (not true in all cases) and there is a shortage of data to support the descriptions. There is an attempt to summarise the main points at the end of the description. Information is evident, but it is not arranged coherently (the description jumps from different usage in general to specific use in different countries, but this does not follow a logical sequence). Without reference back to the individual charts, it is hard to follow the description, especially where reference is also unclear (*it, them, they*). The range of lexis is just adequate for the task (*largest percentage, greatest number, a lot, the second after Asia*), but there is reliance on input material and errors in spelling are noticeable, even where the lexis is supplied in the prompt or the diagrams. A very limited range of structures is used and grammatical errors are frequent (*... all of pie charts have the got ..., ... they almost the second after Asia use water in industrial and opposite of Europe, ... they slightly same in industrial use, ... South Asia and South America are uses the water in Agricultural rather than industrial*). The script represents a mixed profile, but overall achieves Band 4.5.

The charts indicate to five places on the earth. Talking about water and the ways of using it.

It seen obvious all of pie charts have the got the lowest precentage in the domestic uses like at home. However, the largest precentage went with the Agricultural and farms. The center of Asia has the greatest numbers of precentage of Agricultural use. On the other hand in Europe they did not use, water so much as central Asia or Africa. They just use 32,4%. But in the industral they use it alot and the largest precentage with them. If we check on Africa, it seen they almost the second after Asia use water in industrial and opposite of Europe.

In North America and Europe they slightly same in industrial use and just less 4 precentages to Europe, South Asia and South America are uses the water in Agriculturat rather than industrial.

Overall, they all use water much in the farm and Agricultural. Europe and North America they use water more than others in the industrial areas. Africa got the lowest precentage in domestic and industrial uses.

TEST 1, WRITING TASK 2

SAMPLE ANSWER

This is an answer written by a candidate who achieved a **Band 5.5** score. Here is the examiner's comment:

> The candidate puts forward three reasons for why he agrees with the statement and develops/supports the first two of these. Further support and development would be necessary to achieve a higher score here. Organisation is evident, with some simple cohesive devices (sometimes used inaccurately) (*First of all*, *Nowaday*, *At the same time*, *Secondly*, *This*, *However*, *It*, *Finally*, *Overall*), and there are attempts to use paragraphs to present ideas. The range of lexis is generally adequate and appropriate (*pollution*, *driving to work*, *rush hours*, *emissions*, *environment*, *traffic jam*, *congestion*, *public transport*, *commute*, *destinations*, *advantages*, *drawbacks*) and although there are spelling errors, these do not usually impede communication. The candidate attempts to use complex sentences (relative clauses, *if* clauses), but error levels are high and there are also quite frequent errors in punctuation.

In recent years. government focuse on improving quaility of life, that would bring a lot benifits for citizens. Such as. communication, transprotation, health care. Some arguement that built railways is more useful for local people than roads. In my opinion, it is good idea that more train sation is built. There are some reasons.

First of all, it reduced pollution when more people give up driving to work in weekday. Nowaday, people spend a lot of time on the road in rush hours. At the same time, emissions of car bring a pollution in our enviroment. People easily get upset, if they got into traffic jam for longtime. Research has shown that it is get more pollution of air that car stoped on the road without cutting power. Trainstation is a good way to make easy that train never could get into congestion and train is a public transport which is more helpful to reduce air pollution.

Secondly, it solved congestion on the road while many people commute by train, nearly years, a number of car is growing. So, a question that a number of car is over volumed of road is following. This caused traffic jam have being horrible problem. However, the train will take more people to go to their destinations without waiting on road in rush hour. It is more convience for citizen.

Finally, taking public transport is cheaper than privatcal vichele. People could save money to do others they intrested.

Overall, goverment pay more money for building railway. It bring more it is a good decision that advantages than drawbacks.

TEST 2, WRITING TASK 1

SAMPLE ANSWER

This is an answer written by a candidate who achieved a **Band 6** score. Here is the examiner's comment:

> The candidate covers all the key features of the task and rounds off the description with an overview. There is some repetition of information and some irrelevant commentary (*which is good because it shows that more people have learned other languages well*). Information is arranged coherently and there is a clear overall progression, with effective use of cohesive devices, though there is a tendency to rely on dates. The range of vocabulary is adequate for the task, but the writer does not attempt any less common items. There is a mix of simple and complex sentence forms, with a fair degree of accuracy, but the range would need to be wider to achieve a higher score.

The charts show the percentage of the British students, who are able to speak languages other than English, in 2000 and in 2010. In 2000, 20% of the British students were not able to speak another language. But in 2010 the number has decreased to 10%, which is good because it shows that more people have learned other languages well.

The biggest percentage had Spanish only with 30% in 2000. However it has increased by 5% and is in 2010 still the highest percentage with 35%.

In 2000, German only and two other languages were the lowest ones, both with 10%. While in 2010 French only, German only and two other languages show the lowest percentage, while all of them got 10%. All in all, the percentage of German only in 2000 and 2010 hasn't changed. The percentage of French only has decreased by 5%. No other languages percentage was reduced by the half: from the 20% in 2000 to 10% in 2010.

The number of people, who are speaking two other languages has increased by half: In 2000 there were 10% and in 2010 there are 15%.

Another interesting fact is that the percentage of another language has improved aswell: from 15% to 20%.

But still, the most common learned language is Spanish only: In 2000 there were 30% of English students, who spoke it fluently, while in 2010 the number has increased further to 35%.

TEST 2, WRITING TASK 2

SAMPLE ANSWER

This is an answer written by a candidate who achieved a **Band 5** score. Here is the examiner's comment:

> The candidate expresses a position, but only partially addresses the prompt (he or she considers ways in which people can be encouraged to recycle, rather than explicitly looking at the extent to which laws are required); however, ideas are relevant and are supported with clear examples. There is a clear overall progression and cohesive devices are used effectively, if somewhat mechanically (apart from *Either*). Paragraphing is just adequate. Lexical range is adequate for the task and there are attempts to use less common items (*policy, junk bank, citizen, deposit*), but there are errors in word formation (*sale*/sell, *growth*/grow *up*) and some errors in word choice cause difficulty for the reader (*inverse to be some money, motivate advantages of recycling*). There are attempts to use complex sentence structures, but grammatical errors are frequent (*million tons of wastes have been being produced which from home everyday, easy example way to do in house, There is one day a week in order that clean school together which help they have …, Starting give education*).

Nowadays, more than million tons of wastes have been being produced which from home everyday and some people claim that not enough of the litters is recycled. Therefore, they think the governments should have a policy to increase recycling.

It is necessary to say that their governments should take action. For example, providing rubbish bag into each family so that seperate a litter and make it to have value. Many waste; paper, box or steel from home can sale to governments or decrease council tax. Either, the government should provide junk bank that the citizen can deposit recycled waste and inverse to be some money.

Moreover, the government should have spot advertisement on television to motivate advantages of recycling. In Thailand, my country, we have "3R" advertisement standing For reuse, reduce and recycle and easy example way to do in house such as using less plastics bag (reduce), reuse take away box or sale some paper.

In school teacher teach children how to recycle waste at home and go back to tell their parent and come back to report their teacher. There is one day a week in order that clean school together which help they have a good attitud in cleaning.

In conclution, it should be good that the government make some law about waste tax and make people follow the law by give them back some money. Starting give education at school so that when they growth up the will do easier.

In my opinion, it is very easy to government to do as I mention above to reduce waste from homes such as "3R", junk bank, providing rubbish bins and teaching at school and It will be a good habit and good in long term.

TEST 3, WRITING TASK 1

SAMPLE ANSWER

This is an answer written by a candidate who achieved a **Band 6** score. Here is the examiner's comment:

> The candidate has reported all the data in the graph and provides summaries of the main trends (*The production of carbon dioxide in Portugal and Italy was steadily increasing during that period*, *The emission of carbon dioxide in United Kingdom and Sweden was under decrease during that period of time*). There are attempts at comparison (*The emission of carbon dioxide in United Kingdom in 1967 was the highest one among all these 4 countries*, *In 2007 the emission in Sweden was at the same level with Portugal*), but there is some irrelevant material in the final paragraph. There is a clear overall progression, with some use of cohesive devices (*However, in the beginning*). The range of lexis is adequate and appropriate for the task (*production of carbon dioxide, a bit higher, increased, decreased*) and although there are some errors in word choice (*was under decrease, underwent/continued*) and spelling (*tones/tonnes, deacrease*), these do not prevent the message from coming across. There are some attempts to produce complex sentence forms, with good control over grammatical accuracy.

The graph shows the changes in the emission of carbon dioxide in 4 European countries in the period from 1967 to 2007.

The production of carbon dioxide in Portugal and Italy was steadily increasing during that period. In 1967 emission of carbon dioxide in Portugal was approximately 1.3 metric tonnes and in 2007 the emission there achieved 5.4. In Italy in the beginning of the period was a bit higher than 4. However, it increased only till 7.8 by 2007.

The emission of carbon dioxide in United Kingdom and Sweden was under decrease during that period of time. The emission of carbon dioxide in United Kingdom in 1967 was the highest one among all these 4 countries (about 11). But after 1967, it gradually decreased to about 9 metric tones. The emission in Sweden was around 8, 6 metric tones in the beginning, then it steadily increased till 10.5 metric tones. However, in 1977 it got tremendous deacrease in the emission of carbon dioxide which underwent till 2007. In 2007 the emission in Sweden was at the same level with Portugal – around 5.4-5.6.

The changes in emission of carbon dioxide can be connected with the changes in economical development and appearance of some new technologies which reduce emissions.

TEST 3, WRITING TASK 2

SAMPLE ANSWER

This is an answer written by a candidate who achieved a **Band 7** score. Here is the examiner's comment:

> All parts of the prompt are addressed and a clear position is presented throughout the response. Main ideas are extended and supported. Ideas are logically organised and there is a clear progression throughout the response. A range of cohesive devices is used flexibly, while each paragraph has a clear central topic which is developed. The lexical resource is sufficient to allow some flexibility and precision and although there are a few spelling errors, these do not detract from the overall clarity of the response. A variety of complex structures is used with some flexibility and accuracy. Grammar and punctuation are well controlled and error-free sentences are frequent.

Many may say, and I agree, that today's society has almost erased all its boarders and soon will become limitless in what concerns travelling for both work and pleasure. Therefore, if this is to happen, then learning a new language is necessary.

Nowadays, learning a new language for the purpose of working in other countries seems to become more and more popular. Adults in need of money or, why not, recognision are trying to pursue their happiness far away from home. Also, the hey days of employers looking only for capable people have gone. It seems that today's employers are looking not only for multi-skilled employees, but they also want people who know more than their mother tongue. Sooner or later, those who omitted learning more are prone to become jobless.

However, to my mind, a new language shouldn't be learned just for travelling or working in a foreign country. A foreign language should help the learner broaden his mind. By this I mean that the new language should and will allow us to understand more about the world itself, and maybe our ancestors' ways of thinking and acting. Needless to say, knowing another language will help us when it comes to understanding the human race, because language is the first poem of a country.

All of this being said, I believe that learning a different language should be not only for satisfying our physical needs, like money, but also our moral needs, because never before had such a big thirst for knowledge been displayed.

TEST 4, WRITING TASK 1

SAMPLE ANSWER

This is an answer written by a candidate who achieved a **Band 7** score. Here is the examiner's comment:

> The candidate covers the main features of the table and charts, and gives a satisfactory overview of the data. The information is logically organised with a clear progression in the way points are presented. Cohesive devices are used effectively (*during the same two periods*), but not always accurately (*on a contrary*). A range of vocabulary is used flexibly (*shows a negative pattern, illustrates that, an upward trend, has reached its aim*), but there are occasional errors in word choice (*the amount of visitors, It is obviously*). The candidate has used a variety of complex structures (*the charts that show the result of surveys asking people how satisfied they were with their visit, after the refurbishment from 74,000 before the reconstruction to 92,000 after it had been done*). There is good control of grammar, although there are a few minor errors (*there is the charts*). Punctuation is generally well controlled, but full stops are missing at the end of the first and final paragraphs and there are a few minor errors (*lets look*).

The table below shows the amount of visitors to Ashdown Museum during the years after and the year before it was modernized. After the table there is the charts that show the result of surveys asking people how satisfied they were with their visit thos museum, during the same two periods

It is obviously that the numbers of visitors significantly increased after the refurbishment from 74,000 before the reconstruction to 92,000 after it had been done. Now lets look at the charts. The year before refurbishment shows a negative pattern: the results of survey illustrate that only 15% of visitors were very satisfied and the number of dissatisfied people was 40%. The year after refurbishment illustrates that the number of dissatisfied visitors declined and became 15%, on a contrary, people who were very satisfied increased to 35%. Comparing the amount of satisfied visitors we can also see an upward trend (it increased from 30% to 40% after the refurbishment).

To sum up, we can say that all work that has been done to attract new visitors to Ashdown Museum has reached its aim

TEST 4, WRITING TASK 2

SAMPLE ANSWER

This is an answer written by a candidate who achieved a **Band 5.5** score. Here is the examiner's comment:

> All parts of the prompt are addressed and a position is presented (eventually) that is directly relevant to the prompt. Main ideas are relevant, but some are insufficiently developed. Ideas are generally arranged coherently and there is a clear overall progression. Some cohesive devices are used effectively, if mechanically, while others are faulty (*From the point of my view*). Paragraphing is adequate. The lexical resource is limited, but just about adequate for the task. Errors occur in word choice, word formation and spelling (*rise satisfaction*, *the same important as economic for a country*, *morden*) and may cause some difficulty for the reader. The candidate has tried to use a variety of complex structures, but the writing lacks grammatical control (*we are going to talking about*, *A country doesn't have a completed systems is not a completed country* ...). The variety of structures would suggest Band 6 on Grammar, Range and Accuracy, but the errors sometimes impede communication; there are also errors in sentence formation and/ or punctuation (*But some people argue that*, *So the goverments put the economic progress to the top list*, *Because there are other progress such as*).

Nowadays economic progress plays an important part in our life. So many governments believe that it should be the most important goal. But some people argue that it is not the most important thing. There are other progress are equally important. In this essay, we are going to talking about why people have different views.

Generally people think money is everything, if we do not have any money, we can not buy anything. So the goverments put the economic progress to the top list. They believe the if the economic progress could bring a good result, then people can have money to rise satisfaction about their life. However, other types of progress are not important.

Some people suggest that the government should not put the economic progress to the most important place. Because there are other progress such as health system, building design, or education system are the same important as economic for a country. A country doesn't have a completed system is not a completed country, even if it has a lot of money. In this morden society, more and more people realize that money is not the important thing in the world, and it doesn't mean anything, while they think health, happeness are more important than it. Owing to that, some people argue that other types of progress are equally important.

From the point of my view, I agree with that other types of progress are as important as economic. Even though we have a lot of money. we can not buy happeness and health. Therefore the governments should put other types of progress to the important place as well.

Sample answer sheets

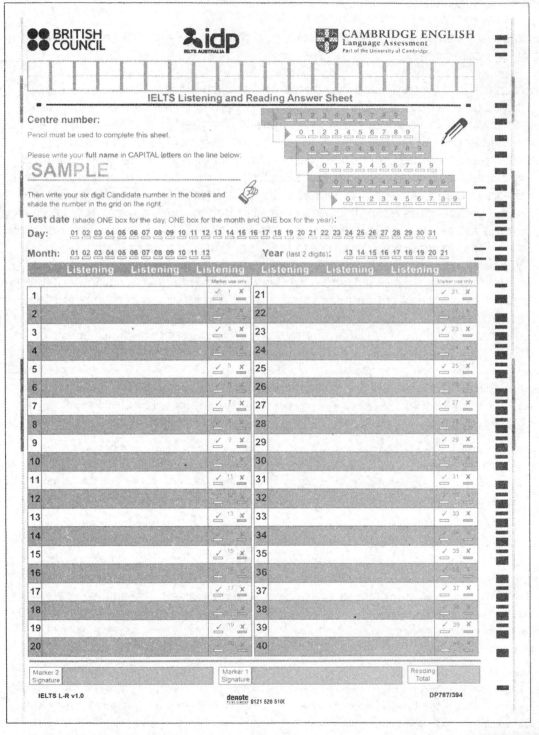

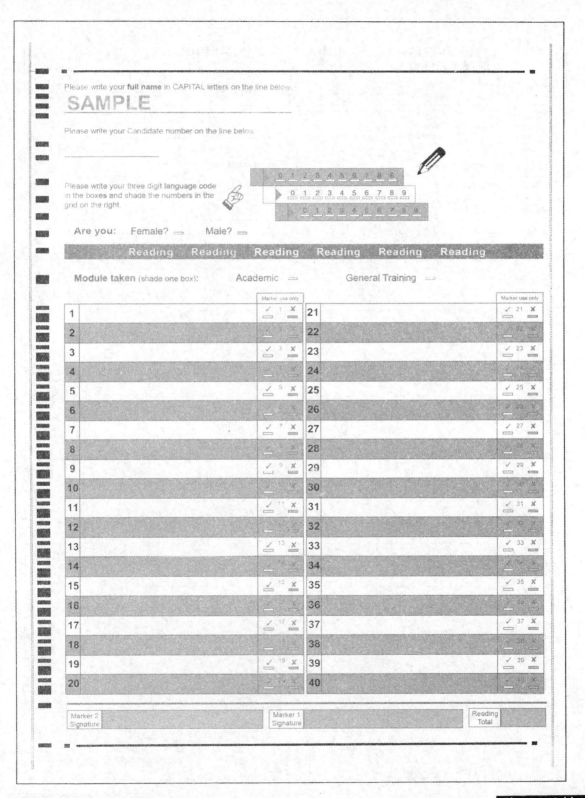

Photocopiable

Sample answer sheets

BRITISH COUNCIL · **idp** IELTS AUSTRALIA · **CAMBRIDGE ENGLISH** Language Assessment Part of the University of Cambridge

IELTS Writing Answer Sheet – TASK 1

Candidate Name

Centre Number

Candidate Number

Module (shade one box): Academic ☐ General Training ☐

Test date

D D M M Y Y Y Y

TASK 1

Do not write below this line

100895/2

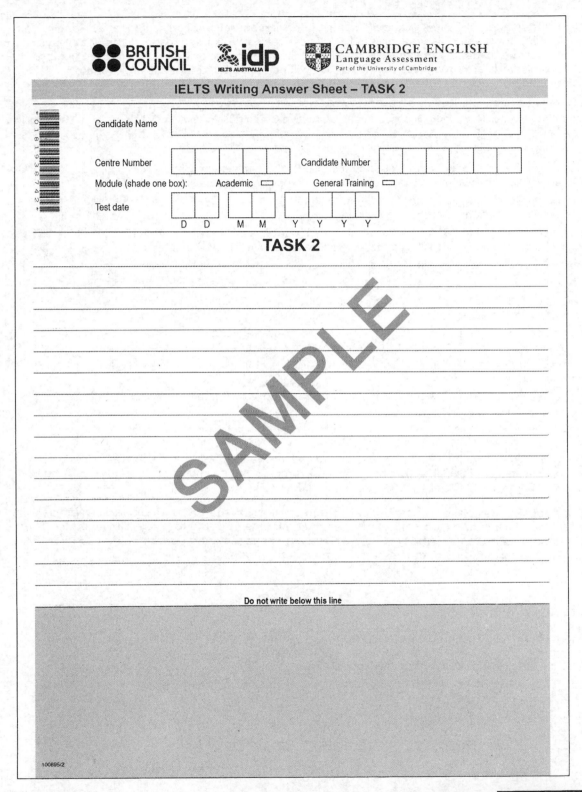

IELTS Writing Answer Sheet – TASK 2

Candidate Name

Centre Number

Candidate Number

Module (shade one box): Academic ☐ General Training ☐

Test date

D D M M Y Y Y Y

TASK 2

Do not write below this line

Acknowledgements

The authors and publishers acknowledge the following sources of copyright material and are grateful for the permissions granted. While every effort has been made, it has not always been possible to identify the sources of all the material used, or to trace all copyright holders. If any omissions are brought to our notice, we will be happy to include the appropriate acknowledgements on reprinting and in the next update to the digital edition, as applicable.

Text on pp. 18–19 adapted from 'The Vertical Farm' by Dickson Despommier, http://www.verticalfarm.com/, licensed under a Creative Commons Attribution 3.0 Unported License;

Text on pp. 21–22 adapted from 'The Falkirk Wheel' with permission from www.scottishcanals.co.uk / www.thefalkirkwheel.co.uk;

Text on pp. 25–26 adapted from 'Reducing the effects of climate change' by Mark Rowe, Nov 2009, *Geographical Magazine*/Syon Publishing. Reproduced with permission;

Text on pp. 46–47 adapted from 'If only they could talk' by Hannah Block, *National Geographic*, © Hannah Block, National Geographic Creative;

Text on pp. 49–50 adapted from 'Neuroaesthetics' by Kat Austen, *New Scientist* 14/07/2012 © 2012 Reed Business Information – UK. All rights reserved. Distributed by Tribune Content Agency.

Text on pp. 65–66 adapted from 'A Short History of Silk in China', Cultural-China;

Text on pp. 65–66 adapted from http://www.demurelook.com/about-silk/silk-history.html, Demure Look;

Text on pp. 69–70 adapted from 'Animal Migrations' by David Quammen, November 2010, *National Geographic Magazine*. Reproduced with permission;

Text on pp. 73–74 adapted from *How the Other Half Thinks*: *Adventures in Mathematical Reasoning* by Sherman Stein, 2001, Dover Publications. Reproduced with permission of Sherman Stein;

Graph on p. 77 adapted from 'CO^2 emissions in Europe' by World Bank. Copyright © 2014 by Google. Reproduced with permission;

Text on pp. 87–88 adapted from 'A Thing or Two about Twins' by Peter Miller, January 2012, *National Geographic Magazine*. Reproduced with permission;

Text on pp. 91–92 adapted from 'Introduction to film sound' by Jane Knowles Marshall. http://www.filmsound.org/marshall/index.htm

Text on pp. 97–98 adapted from *The Unfolding of Language*: *The Evolution of Mankind's Greatest Invention* by Guy Deutscher, copyright 2005, 2006, Arrow Books, an imprint of Random House and Henry Holt and Company, LLC. All rights reserved. Reproduced with permission.

The publisher has used its best endeavours to ensure that the URLs for external websites referred to in this book are correct and active at the time of going to press. However, the publisher has no responsibility for the websites and can make no guarantee that a site will remain live or that the content is or will remain appropriate.

ERRATUM 勘误

Page 32: In the 8th line from the bottom, "advantates" should be "advantages".

第32页：倒数第8行，**advantates**应为**advantages**。

Page 131: Correct answers to questions 9, 19 and 21-26 should be:

第131页：9、19、21-26题的正确答案如下：

9	B	19	TRUE	21	NOT GIVEN	22	TRUE
23	FALSE	24	C	25	A	26	E